S0-HJO-638

PRAISE FOR THE MAN IS GREATER THAN THE BRAND

"Richard's vulnerability and transparency are woven in throughout this book. Society often places pressure on men to conform to a certain masculine ideal, which can lead to a lack of authenticity. Yeargin calls out and challenges toxic behaviors—safeguarding men against trauma and underachievement."

— ASA T. BRIGGS, DNP, CEO AND FOUNDER OF BRIGGS PSYCHIATRY AND BEHAVIORAL HEALTH, PC

"We often let people's perception of who they think we should be based on where we come from, how we look, and what we sound like dictate how we show up in the world. In doing so, we neglect our own journey of self-discovery, talent discovery, and personal development. From a somewhat troubled high schooler to a nationally renowned football player—Richard shares the expectations that he and others placed on him as well as relationships and circumstances that were working behind the scenes."

— RYAN SCHACHTNER, CEO OF A MUST WIN

"Richard is one of the most dynamic men that I have met. It goes without saying that he's athletically gifted, but he's much more than that. I met Richard while speaking at a Speaking Bootcamp in Orlando. My first impression was *why was a man this accomplished studying to get better?* This goes to the character of a man who puts his soul into his work. His will propels him to his goal. Richard has a story to tell, and when he speaks it, you will listen. His presence and speech are commanding and I hung on to every word he spoke. Life is not pre-determined, but I can say with confidence that Richard will accomplish anything he sets in his path."

— JOSEPH MILLER, NATIONAL SALES MANAGER AT CSAT SOLUTIONS LP

"Richard opened up his heart to us in this book, sharing his hardships and how he came out on top. His stories are intended to help you repair yourself, trusting that the best is yet to come. Everyone needs a coach, both on the field and off. Richard's book provides the course reset we all need, like a trusted coach guiding us through life."

— JOSHUA BEEKMAN, DIRECTOR OF FOOTBALL INITIATIVES AT BOSTON COLLEGE

THE MAN IS GREATER THAN THE BRAND

SHEDDING PAST BROKENNESS TO LIVE AS KINGS AND QUEENS

RICHARD YEARGIN III, MS

STREAMLINE BOOKS

THE MAN IS GREATER THAN THE BRAND

Shedding Past Brokenness to Live as Kings and Queens

Copyright © 2023 by Richard Yeargin III

All rights reserved.

No part of this book may be reproduced, distributed, or transmitted in any form or by any means, including photocopying, recording, or other electronic or mechanical methods, without the written permission from the author, except in the case of brief quotations embodied in a book review.

Scriptures taken from the Holy Bible, New International Version®, NIV®. Copyright © 1973, 1978, 1984, 2011 by Biblica, Inc.™ Used by permission of Zondervan. All rights reserved worldwide. www.zondervan.com The "NIV" and "New International Version" are trademarks registered in the United States Patent and Trademark Office by Biblica, Inc.™

Cover design by Will Severns

Streamline Books

www.WriteMyBooks.com

Paperback ISBN: 9-798-3905-0300-3

Hardcover ISBN: 9-798-3924-0810-8

May 1st, 2023

To my beloved wife Kayla, my dear son Elijah, and my sweet daughter Madison: thank you for making my life meaningful and purposeful. Everyday I strive to be the best version of myself in the image and likeness of the creator to better serve you all as the gifts that I have been blessed with. I hope when you read this it engraves in your mind and your heart a new meaning for understanding your why in order to fully unlock your potential.

CONTENTS

M > B

FOREWORDS

BY ANTOINE MCCLAIN & FLOYD S. "TREY" MILLS III

From the Desk of:

Antoine Mcclain, Clemson University Director of PAW Journey - OVERTIME

As we all live and maneuver through this journey called life, two things are for certain: we all will experience transitions, and we all will experience death. The sooner we digest and fully accept the reality of those two things, the better we become at navigating "The Pivot" that will take place. We all can get so consumed with life and being in our groove that any ounce of inconvenience or change shakes up our lives in such a matter that sends us into a very dark space of confusion, self-doubt, or worthlessness.

The dark space is not the time to retreat or wave the white flag, but it is the time to show self-discipline, perseverance, and the principles and morals we have developed over the course of our lives.

I truly believe that God sends us tests or disruptions in our lives to make us aware of the changes we need to make, to get our attention, or to see if we are serious about the things we are praying and asking for. He is also checking our faith and our attitude.

On the contrary, not every mishap should be looked at as a test, but as an opportunity to practice all the things that will push us closer to our goals. We cannot predict what will happen to us or how people will choose to treat us. But what we may fail to realize is that every mishap gives us power because, although we cannot control life or other people's thoughts and actions, we can control our mindset and attitude. Having a great and positive mind can give you the edge to surpass setbacks or that "thing" coming to an end.

On the road of transition or things coming to an end, we find ourselves in that "dark place" before we get to the other side. In that dark place, four words will forever serve us if we fully believe in them as we say them: "This too shall pass." In the midst of confusion and doubt, when you are unsure if you will ever find hope and victory, remember, "This too shall pass." When you fear pivoting to something new because you feel inadequate because it's new territory, and it will make you very uncomfortable, "This too shall pass." When you are worried about how you will make ends meet because you must rebuild all over again, "This too shall pass." Developing a "This too shall pass" mindset will allow you to open your heart and mind to acknowledge your circumstance and provide you with a positive mindset that great things are ahead of you.

Transitions help us to build character and force us to thrive in being uncomfortable. What my good friend Richard Yeargin has written in this book provides a roadmap for building character for long-term success. However, I want this "Foreword" to serve as somewhat of a warning: if stepping out of your comfort zone scares you, pass this book along to someone else.

Whenever things come to an end and we are forced to transition, we must keep pushing because the world and our responsibility will still be there. Transition teaches us good habits and discipline because whether we feel comfortable or uncomfortable, happy or sad, motivated or not, we must continue to live life and see every bit of it as an opportunity to thrive.

From the Desk of:
Floyd S. "Trey" Mills III, Attorney at Trammell & Mills

I FIRST MET RICHARD back in the Spring of 2015 when Clemson's Athletic Department reached out to our law firm about a young, bright athlete who wanted to get some exposure to law and make some money in the off-season legitimately working, before the time of the Name Image Likeness policy. Embracing him was like hugging a brick wall and he sure did have the "Gift of Gab," along with an outgoing personality. However, much of that personality he presented to new acquaintances was a façade. I was quick to call him out and let him know I had his best intentions at heart but he was going to have to work. Being an athlete may have garnered him wonderful things on campus, but off campus he was someone I was paying hourly and I expected to work. My stance was in direct conflict with our older partner in the firm who would gladly pay him hourly to learn about the ins and outs of practice and what was going on inside the world of Clemson Football. This was during a time in Clemson Football when National Championships (plural) were on the horizon and it was the heyday of Clemson athletes, students, and fans alike. Richard was no doubt reaping the benefits of being a great athlete for a program that was about to bring home two additional National Championships. I knew his goal, like most athletes' goal, was to play in the NFL. And why wouldn't it be, given the fact he was groomed throughout his life with private schools wanting him to come be part of their student body and—more importantly—their football team? He helped me see the "other side" of athletics that I would have never been privy to without pushing him to show me the real Richard Yeargin. We then started having more meaningful discussions about how he could advance as a student-athlete and benefit from all the opportunities he was presented.

Unfortunately, I remember well the night he called in a panic because he had just been involved in a car accident, flipping over and fracturing his cervical vertebrae. Had he not had a tree trunk as a neck, he would be dead or a paraplegic. His hard work and efforts to get back into and continue to compete in Division 1 athletics at Clemson and then Boston College are no doubt impressive. However, it came at a price to his mental, emotional and psychological well-being. Plus, I knew his NFL dreams were even more statistically impossible than they had first been at his prime. He continued to work towards his dream but then he was hit with another uncontrollable factor in life: the COVID-19 Pandemic. Not the best time for an injured athlete's come back when you are doing Zoom calls with NFL teams. As he confided at one point, he was already a "Black Sheep" of an athlete being publicly injured but COVID put the nail in the coffin for his NFL dreams. We started deepening our relationship during this dark time in his life.

Richard finally had to come to terms with what so many others before him have had to realize: all he had worked for, been groomed for, and been adored for was about to come to an end. The real Richard Yeargin was about to step out from the cloak of football fame, adoration, and paid higher education. He was finally going to have to use that degree, and his small world of Clemson's campus was about to open up to the world. It was a slap in the face that I had warned him would come one day, a realization that the "Gravy Train" has ended. Scholarships are gone, NFL moved on, and now is the time in your life you become . . . like the rest of us. Except you are not like the rest of us because you have exemplified discipline throughout your life as a high-level athlete, been courted by Division I programs, and played Division I football at a high level. Use that to your advantage and milk the opportunities out of that rich background of success. He fought it at first and had to go down some rabbit holes that only helped him chisel away at his foundation and forge the man that he is becoming. Real-world responsibilities with long-term relationships and children certainly have a way of accelerating that development. I am proud of the man he is becoming after football and even prouder of the opportunities he has embraced, knowing all of life is like a "game." You just have to know your opponent and the rules of the game to ensure you win it.

Richard Yeargin will win the game, so listen and enjoy what he has to offer to anyone that is open to learning, listening, and being prepared for their game when it presents itself.

M > B

INTRODUCTION

The summer rain drummed on the gas station awning in Greenville, South Carolina. I stood by my 2010 midnight blue Honda Civic, filling up a final tank before driving back to Clemson University. I peered through the sheets of rain, watching the water stream from the parking lot into ravines along the road.

"It's just rain," I thought. "I'll be fine."

As a senior in college, my redshirt and rookie days were behind me. I was finally considered a first string defensive end destined for greatness. I had endured blistering workouts and Coach Dabo Swinney's fervid player character development. It was my time to shine. I was getting ready to enter my final season where reps would not be shared amongst my teammates as much.

It was all me, or so I thought. I was patient, or so it seemed. I had worked hard according to the expectations placed on me. I truly felt like I deserved it ALL. We had just won the national championship in January 2017, and I had just considered which agent I would sign with. So it was safe to say, I was on the all-star track to the NFL.

I jumped into my car and pulled onto the highway. As I rode down I-85 south towards Clemson, I came upon construction. I hit the brakes hard, trying to slow down in time. My wheels locked, and next thing I knew, I had lost control of the car. I felt myself tumbling upside down. The car rolled over twice before settling on the side of the road.

The moments afterward blur together, but I remember seeing strangers walking up to my car, calling 911. I reached for my phone and called my brother. I wanted my family to hear about the accident from me before hearing from someone else.

I was rushed to the hospital, where they found that I had broken three vertebrae in my neck and suffered a concussion. Because of the fractures in my neck, I was put on watch for paralysis and forced to remain immobile for three days. If I ever did play football again—and that was a big IF—it would be at least another year according to medical experts.

Each of us depends on something for value. For identity. For purpose. My value came from football. My team at Clemson University had just won a national championship, and we were planning on winning again the following season.

The car wreck completely blindsided me. When Joe Mixon blindsided me in the 2015 Orange Bowl freshman year, I let him know what's up. I could push back. But this blindside cracked me down to my core like an apple.

In the coming chapters, you'll hear more about the days after the accident—the injuries, the recovery, the second injury, and the second recovery. You'll hear about the shattering of all my NFL dreams and what it took to rebuild a new life after football. But this book isn't about me. It's about you. When life blindsides you, and the goals you hoped for disappear right before your eyes, what do you have left? Who are you?

In this life we are so consumed with brands. I define brands as anything we find or place our identity in. When I played for Clemson, people saw the brand. They saw a football star with a championship win. After my car wreck, people no longer saw the brand but a casualty. Two years after my accident, when I transitioned over to play at Boston College, I adopted a new brand. I became the comeback player. But who was I really? Did my identity change, or just my circumstances? How do you let go of an identity that you once were but no longer can be?

In the pages ahead, you'll hear my story, both from my perspective and the perspectives of those closest to me. I have chosen these five people to share their life lessons because no one is a self-made man. You'll read about my life from the view of my brother, from Clemson football Head Coach Dabo Swinney, from CEOs Billy Milam and Joe Gasque, and of course from my beloved wife, Kayla Yeargin. The people who surround us shape who we are. I would not have made it through life without them.

I have divided my life story into three sections: the boy, the man, and the king. I follow Coach Chris Crumpler and Chae Powell's podcast "Boy Man King" and recently attended their King Conference. These life stages perfectly summarize the goals of each person's journey. We all start somewhere, but we can't afford to stay there. We must mature from childhood to adulthood, and then move into full ownership of our true potential. Each one of us, whether a college athlete or not, must ask what our lives are made of. I come at my story from the experiences of an athlete, but the lessons apply to all walks of life.

The rules of college sports have changed, as name, image and likeness rules shift and players are now allowed to monetize their athletic careers. Now more than ever, the spotlight comes earlier and players are pressured to become a brand as well as a student. They need to focus not only on their education but on their brand presence. Yet is this where the focus should be? What protections do we set up for ourselves to ensure we aren't carried away? Whether you're a high school or college athlete, or simply someone wanting to hear the story of a comeback kid, I hope you take away a renewed purpose and vision for who you are becoming.

Dr. Martin Luther King Jr. once said, "The ultimate measure of a man is not where he stands in moments of comfort and convenience, but where he stands at times of challenge and controversy." Throughout the book, you will notice that I share the stories not of winning state and national championships, but of struggle and loss. I have found, as Dr. King did and as you will too in your own life, that we are forged not in comfort but in the fire.

I hope as you read, you gain vision for your life. You have a purpose beyond how you perform or how many people cheer you on from the sidelines. Who you are is greater than what you do. Your inner man is greater than your outer brand.

PART I

THE BOY

CHAPTER 1
MORALS

M > B

The worst year of my life wasn't the year of the accident. It wasn't the year I lost my track to the NFL. The worst year of my life came in third grade, when my grandma passed away in my arms mid-conversation.

You can't imagine a closer relationship than what I had with my grandma. I went to her house every day after school. I would sprawl on her living room floor doing homework, then help her with dinner in the kitchen. She often cooked enough to feed my parents, aunts, uncles, and cousins. I still remember the smells of smothered pork chops, macaroni and cheese, black-eyed peas, and cornbread wafting across her house. Laughter would fill the house as family members poured into the dining room to fill their stomachs. To be in her home meant to be safe and cared for. She was the magnet that drew our family together and the pillar that strengthened our community.

One week, I went with my aunts to Illinois to see my older cousin Sam whom I always admired and truly looked up to while he played football at Illinois State University. While we were there, my aunt received the call that grandma had a stroke.

My Uncle Charles had gone over to her house and smelled food burning. He found her collapsed in her backyard. But no one told me. People didn't talk. I just saw the panicked rush as we tried to get home. We pulled up to the hospital, and I didn't realize what had happened till I saw her on the hospital bed.

She remained in hospice for several months, and I tagged along with my dad to visit her every day–either before he went to work or during his lunch break. I stopped going to school, and my brother drove back from college. I blamed myself. If only I had been there and not in Illinois, I would have been at her house when the stroke happened. I could have called 911 and prevented the hours she lay unconscious in her backyard.

I was sitting by her bedside when she whispered, "I love you," and breathed for the last time.

If I could have traded my life for Grandma's life, I would have in a heartbeat. She wasn't just a community pillar; she was my pillar. When she died, part of me died with her.

Loss forces you to reevaluate life. When the pillar you leaned on crumbles, what is left to support you? I realized I didn't have ground to stand on either, just an empty hole where she had been.

I found Christ in the third grade, mostly as an attempt to fill the hole my grandma had left behind. I used to go to church with her every Wednesday and Sunday just to be in her presence. I'll admit after she died, I chose to follow Christ only because I thought he would make my life easier. But instead, it got even harder. See, at that time as a boy, I was naive to what "having faith" really meant. I had to rent my grandma's faith in order to press on and possess my own meaning of faith in my attempt at becoming a man. She left behind her greatest gift—faith—and bestowed it upon me as a form of inheritance from being so close with her. Now I decided I didn't just want to watch people drink from the cup. I wanted to drink myself.

Three years later, the 2008 recession hit. At the same time, my dad received a cancer diagnosis and began treatments. My mother's beauty & cosmetology business service struggled as clients diminished and she struggled to keep her business afloat. My parents could no longer afford to keep me enrolled in a private school, so I started public school.

In Fort Lauderdale, railroad tracks separate the good from the bad. East of the tracks lies the beachfront property. Valuable. Wealthy. Drive west of the tracks and you'll hit the inner city. Crime. Drugs. My school was on the wrong side of the tracks.

Switching from private to public school jolted me into an awakening I wasn't ready for. I went to a public middle school with the neighborhood kids from Two-Seven as we called it (Twenty-Seventh Street in Eastgate, a subdivision of Lauderdale Lakes). I was with all the neighborhood kids night and day. Fifteen- and sixteen-year-olds went to my school, having failed a couple years and gotten held back. Those kids lived in an entirely different life stage. They were about to start driving. So I, as an eleven-year-old, received exposure to activities far beyond my age. Drugs. Fights. Administrators having affairs with students. The gangs would designate certain days to beat up students from different nationalities. If you didn't hang with the right crowd, you were liable to be their next target.

My one life goal became simple: survival. No matter what it costs, be on the top. In order to survive, I had to be accepted by the right crowd. In order to be cool, I had to start skipping school.

I entered that school in sixth grade under their magnet program of pre-law. By seventh grade, I was kicked out of the program. My grades had plummeted. I started smoking dope and shooting dice. We started out just skipping lunch. Then it became classes. By eighth grade, I was labeled an at-risk student. I was the dope dealer, selling weed in the hallway to the other kids. In two years, I had spiraled down from the accelerated program into a "disengaged learner"

> Now I decided I didn't just want to watch people drink from the cup. I wanted to drink myself.

as our school put it. Has my intelligence level changed? No. But my morals sure had.

My parents really had no idea the type of risks and mischief I was into. I lived a completely double life at home versus when I was at school with my peers. What did morals matter when I was focusing on survival?

While I was in middle school, I couldn't see beyond the danger of daily life. Not to use this as an excuse for my behavior, but my environment completely reshaped who I was. At age fourteen, I had no vision for my life beyond surviving each school day. I had completely forsaken my faith.

A Way Out

My first wake-up call came one Saturday. I had a writing class to prepare for Florida's standardized testing. It was a collaborative class, with three or four teachers to help all of us with learning how to respond to writing prompts. The students would bounce ideas off of each other as they worked together.

Well, I was not about that life on a Saturday. I turned in my paper and left that class.

I later heard from another friend who had stayed in class that one of the teachers started going through the responses. When she got to my paper, she was impressed with it, but I had left without putting my name on it. She asked the class, "Who wrote this paper?" My friend knew it was mine because we had been sharing our ideas with each other as we worked.

"Well, if he would ever put his name on his paper and show up to class, he might be something someday," the teacher said.

Meanwhile, as my friend and I left the school building and headed to the parking lot, a security guard spotted us and started chasing after us. We sprinted to the gate and got the heck out of dodge before she could reach us; then we booked it down the block. I kid you not, as I ran from the guard, I thought, "That's like God trying to chase me down." Even as a kid, I knew what I was doing was wrong. I knew I had left my name off my paper. I felt like God was saying to me, "Come back and claim what's yours." As I ran, that voice pounded with my footsteps, "You left. You didn't put your name on it. You left. Why? Why didn't you stay?"

I had literally left my gift behind and run from it.

Luckily, even when we're running, God always gives us a way back. Once my buddy and

I had run a safe distance from the school, we slowed down and got ready to light up a blunt. At that moment, down the road drove a familiar van. My father. The school must have phoned my parents, because he was out looking for us. He just happened to drive down the exact street we were on. My buddy recognized the van and instantly ran away. My dad pulled over, jumped out, and caught up with me.

All my friends respected my dad. He drove us around. He did so much for us. He was a beacon of hope to all and a phenomenal human being. He gave so much leeway for me to live my life—although he could be stern when he needed to. But he wanted to let me live and experience things, and then he would correct me later if he needed to. He didn't yell at me or beat me, but if I messed up, he was there for me.

That day made it real. As soon as we got back in the van, he asked, "What are you doing?" He couldn't believe I had been skipping school.

I thought I had gotten away with cheating, but that day made me realize I was only cheating myself. I thought I could get the right result by doing the wrong action, but I had no idea how I was only harming myself.

How God Gets Our Attention

I recently came across a Facebook post that sparked my interest because it perfectly described what I've been through in life. The post, by TEAM3 Ministries, summarized an Andy Stanley teaching, "How God Gets Our Attention."[1] I always thought of God speaking through the Bible and sermons, but the post highlighted how God speaks to us in ways outside of the box we put Him in.

The post listed four specific ways God can speak to us:

1. A restless spirit
2. An unsolicited word from another person
3. Unusual circumstances
4. Unanswered prayers

Can you relate? Take the first one for example, "a restless spirit." I felt this restlessness at different times in my life. I noticed it when I was younger. I had a nagging sense, "Is this what life is? This can't be it. There's got to be more." When my grandma passed away, the hole she left in my life was an opportunity for God to fill me later. I didn't realize the empty feeling was His way of calling me to Himself. This empty feeling followed me all the way from middle school to my college years. I had a God-sized void that only He could fill. I began hanging out with the wrong crowds and taking on new identities that were never intended for me. I turned to drugs, girls, and parties, all to try and fill this hole. These things were never enough. They could never fully satisfy me. I was restless. Always trying to figure out ways to get more. I even tried to fill this void with football. But God kept showing me over and over again that the answer I was in search of was him all along. Only he could satisfy me and give me that peace I was in need of. All the other things were temporary highs, but God was the only constant. During the restless months after my car accident, when I was bedridden, God's voice came through loud and clear: I had to surrender to his plan, not mine.

Take the second item on the list, "an unsolicited word from another person." All those times my teachers and parents were giving me advice, trying to keep me on the right track–those were times God was speaking to me through them. And I could go on–I had unusual life circumstances through the wreck and unanswered prayers for God to heal me on my timeline. All the while, I didn't realize his goal was for me to start listening to him.

What about you?

Where do you see these four areas reflected in your life? If you keep feeling restless, if you keep receiving advice that you aren't wanting to hear, if you face life circumstances different from what you expected, and if you feel frustrated God's not answering your prayers on your timeline–God might be trying to get your attention. Take the time to slow down and listen.

Reflection Questions

1. What is your environment? Who are you hanging out with? Is your environment shaping you for the better?
2. How is God trying to get your attention? What would it mean for you to stop and listen to him?
3. What gifts do you know you possess but still have yet to put your name on?

CHAPTER 2
RESPECT
WITH MY BROTHER, RICHARD YEARGIN II

Richard Yeargin II: *In fifth grade, I asked my parents for a brother. Tired of being an only child, I longed for the camaraderie my friends enjoyed. Every time I went to hang with my cousins, I saw they each had their partner in crime. I played with them outnumbered, one-on-two or more. No one played on my team.*

I went to my parents and said, "Everybody else has a brother or sister, so what am I going to do when y'all die? Who's going to be here for me? Who's going to fight for me?" At eleven years old, I asked them specifically for a brother.

They made it happen. In 1996, Richard Yeargin III

entered the world. He shared my first, middle, and last name, and everything else in life.

I was the kind of kid who always took care of my stuff. I kept my room tidy. I got good grades. I tried to be the good kid. So when Little Rich came along, I accepted him as my responsibility. I had asked for him, so I took care of him. He was always on my hip. Even in high school, I remember driving home from a friend's house at 1:00 a.m. with Little Rich in the back seat.

When I left for college, I didn't get accepted to the football team from the start. I had to walk on. Then after college, I found a job at State Farm. I worked two years in Illinois and then transferred back home to live with my family and work in Fort Lauderdale. I had heard from my parents that Little Rich wasn't doing well. That weighed on me. I had asked for him, and I felt responsible to see him succeed. I called Little Rich and told him I was coming home in six months and he had better get his act together.

At twenty-six years old, I moved back in with my parents.

I knew all the mistakes I had made. I didn't want Little Rich to do the same.

I had tried to make it in college football, thinking I could just play for my high school like the average kid and that would be enough. When no colleges wanted me on their team, I found out the hard way I had to work my way in. I had to convince people to want me. Now, two years after playing college football, I knew better. I knew Little Rich still had a chance at colleges wanting him, but we had to make it happen.

I put him through the equivalent of a pledge period. When I arrived, I asked him, "Do you want to play football?"

"Yes," he replied.

"Do you want to be the best?"

"Yes."

"Then you will," I told him. "You will have the respect of your peers, of coaches, of the school—but you'll have to work for it."

So we began. He had no option to fail. No option to quit. After his high school team's workouts, he'd find me in the school weight room waiting for him to finish with his team's workouts so we could begin ours.

I never asked him to do anything I didn't do myself. I knew that for him to respect me, he needed to know I was in the process with him, working as hard as he worked or harder. Every lift, I lifted with him. Every drill, I ran with him. I lay on the workout bench sweating beside him, and we figured it out together. What I wished I had received in high school, I gave to him. If we want respect, we have to earn it by walking alongside someone in their struggle.

When my brother came back home to live with us, I didn't want the discipline and structure he brought with him. Sure, I wanted to win at football. But I thought I had already achieved that. I was on the team as a freshman at a prestigious private school. I hadn't seen what my brother had seen, regarding what it would take to make it to the next level. I had to walk by faith, not by sight, trusting he had already been where I wanted to be. I had to trust that if I did everything he told me to do, I would succeed.

Respect came slowly.

I remember one time running preseason drills on Memorial Day. My brother and I were at the high school, but no one else from the team was practicing. There he was on the practice field—the college athlete running drills like his life depended on it. He sprinted fast and on point. Then I ran the same drill, but in slow motion compared to him, huffing and puffing all the way. I was only half-trying, and he knew it.

After the third time showing me the drill and watching my halfhearted runs, he grew frustrated. We fell into a knock-down, drag-out fight that day. He whooped me, and I took it like a man. I needed it.

Another time, I went out with friends on Halloween night. We decided to throw eggs on some cars. Unfortunately, one of the cars we egged happened to be an unmarked cop car. The cop got out and told us we could be arrested on the spot—handcuffed and taken to jail.

Thankfully, she decided to go easy on us. She called our parents to come pick us up. Next thing I knew, my brother showed up.

"Man, what are you doing?" he said when he

arrived. The whole drive home, he lit into me, swearing up and down from A to Z. When we got home, the lecture continued. As painful as that was, I would much rather go home with my brother than get carted off in the paddy wagon. I knew he cared and was in it with me.

Respect includes firstly respecting yourself, then respecting others, and then earning their respect. The key to respect is how you live. Be disciplined, dedicated, and undistracted.

Disciplined—When you're young, discipline comes from outward motivators. But eventually, your discipline must come from within. My brother made me do every workout. He kept me in line and stopped me from dealing drugs. But after I went off to college, I was on my own. What's more, I went to the top of my team as a senior to the bottom in college. I redshirted as a freshman, and it got to me. I spiraled again. I started doing drugs. I called my brother one day. When I was at the bottom, I called the man who had been in the trenches with me every day.

"Rich," he said, "I told you that someday you'll have to fight for yourself, and this is it. You've got to decide to dig deep and fight back."

I had to internalize the discipline he had

instilled. Only then could other people respect me—after I respected myself.

Dedicated—If you say you'll be there, then be there. Show up. My brother proved himself to be the most dedicated person I knew in my early years, and he taught me how to do the same. Most people say, "Put yourself in someone else's shoes." My brother did that for me, and then some. When he saw I didn't know how to tie my shoes, he taught me how. When I tripped on my own shoelaces, he picked me back up.

If he asked me to do a workout, I heard him breathing heavily beside me, sweating next to me. He never asked me to do anything unless he did it with me. He earned my respect by showing up. Every day. He never gave up on me, and seeing his dedication gave me a deep respect for him.

Undistracted—Know your goals, and then stay focused on how you'll reach them. We often think of being undistracted as in staying focused on reaching our goals. But we don't often take time to think about *how* we're reaching those goals. How you reach your goals is as important as what you're reaching for.

Many times people ask, "What's one more thing I can get out of this person?" They live in a one-up mentality, trying to use others to advance themselves. Don't live that way. Guard your heart. Yes, be competitive and try to succeed, but don't do it at the cost of your integrity. When you start using people, you get off course. Be aware and vigilant in how you live.

As you strive to earn others' respect, you must respect yourself first. When I was at my lowest in college, I had to learn that I was the only one who could fight for myself. I was the only one who could choose to stay disciplined, dedicated, and undistracted. I received respect from my brother because he taught me how to live differently from everyone around me so that I'd get different results than everyone around me.

Once you respect yourself, then you can respect others. Don't demand that they respect you. In order to earn their respect, you have to give it first. Live with self-discipline. Show them your dedication. Don't get distracted in how you pursue your goals. My brother did all these things for me, and even though I didn't like his discipline at the time, I grew to respect him for it. Learning to live with respect opened the door for manners, which opened a door for me.

Respect Means Manners

Each of us has a room we want to enter. A classroom. A locker room. A boardroom. Each room has an entry. Not just anyone can enter. The threshold sets the expectation. What room are you trying to enter? How do you arrive? And more importantly, how do you stay?

Manners are more than opening the door for someone. Manners will open the door for you.

My first day of kindergarten, I stepped into the classroom and faced the meanest lady I had ever met. My parents had enrolled me in a private school in Fort Lauderdale, Florida, run by Caribbean women who knew the meaning of discipline. I sat frozen to my plastic chair, certain that my teacher would snap my head off if I ever dared to ask her a question.

This became a problem by the end of the day because I needed to use the facilities but dreaded raising my hand. I sat still. I had an accident, right there on my first day of kindergarten class.

Thankfully, my teacher wasn't actually the meanest lady in the world. She swooped in, took me to the boys' room, cleaned me up, gave me a fresh set of clothes, and led me back into the classroom. No one laughed at me. Everyone showed kindness. It was just another day in the life of a kindergarten class. Yet I dumped shame on myself.

But this story isn't about me. It's about my mom, Janice Yeargin, and how she showed up for my teacher.

Manners are more than opening the door for someone. Manners will open the door for you.

My mom picked me up that day and instantly noticed the new outfit. "Why are you wearing a different set of clothes than when I dropped you off?" she asked, and the story spilled out. "Richard," she said, "if you need help, just raise your hand."

My mom became best friends with that teacher. She came inside and chatted with her. My mom ran a beauty salon, and she invited my kindergarten teacher to drop by. Eventually my mom became her hairdresser. To this day, she remains a family friend.

I was late to school nearly every day. My teachers didn't mind though. They knew we were late because my mom was swinging by Publix, the local grocery store, and buying coffee, donuts, and fruit for all the teachers. They loved her. She showed up for them in a way that made them feel cared for and seen. And she taught me that the first step of manners is asking for help.

The Importance of Manners

What room do you want to enter? Wherever you're trying to get, I'll give you a secret: you don't have to be the smartest person to get into the room. But in order to stay in the room, you have to have manners. You have to be a good human being. I will burst your bubble right now —I'm not the smartest person. Or the most talented. Or the most athletic. I will never claim to be. But I can still treat every person with honor.

When you walk into a room, what presence do you carry? Who you think you are and how people actually perceive you might be vastly different. We commonly think of manners as the basics—saying please and thank you, opening the door for someone, or offering a coat. But at the heart, manners simply mean how you show up for people.

I first learned manners from my grandma, Margaret Yeargin. I spent many days with her, and many nights—cooking in her kitchen, lying on her living room floor with homework projects spread out in front of me, and going to church with her every Wednesday and Sunday. As I spent all that time around her, I watched as people gravitated toward her. Looking back, I realize she drew people in not because she was an older lady with experience raising kids, but because of her manners. She taught me the three most important lessons about showing up for people: be aware, be intentional, and always execute at a high level.

Be Aware—Do you notice others' needs around you? Before manners can be about what you do, they have to be about what you see. You can't offer to open a door for someone until you see them walking up with their hands full. You can't offer your chair until you see the older person standing and realize that person needs the chair more than you do. We can make up a long list of dos and don'ts and call them manners, but at the heart of manners is first off being aware. See others' needs.

Be Intentional—If the first step is to see the need, the next step is to take action on it. It's one thing to notice a person is cold. Nearly anyone can do that. But if we stop at the observation and don't offer them our coat, awareness is worthless. Intentionality bridges the gap between awareness and manners. Take notice, and then take action. Once you see the need, ask yourself, "What can I do to help?"

My mom saw the teachers at my school showing up early day after day to be there when students arrived. She saw their need for acknowledgment, care, and honor. She saw teachers hold an often thankless role. And she acted on that need. Did it cost her? Sure. Intentionality always costs. We offer something we have to meet someone else's need—whether it's food, kindness, time, or a smile. Intentionality takes time, and it takes extra effort.

Always Execute at a High Level—All through high school and college, coaches always saw me as a leader. They saw me in that light not because I was the most talented on the team, but because I showed up as a player and student of the game in a way that made others want to follow me.

Manners opened doors for me.

Executing at a high level doesn't mean being the best; it means trying the hardest. I had a teachable spirit. I made the extra effort to connect with coaches and teachers on a personal level. I asked for tips. I honored my fellow athletes. I didn't insist on being the expert because I already knew I wasn't. My grandma had taught me to look at myself critically instead of judging someone else, and I carried that attitude with me.

Are You Ready for the Challenge?

Living with respect for yourself and others will draw attention to you. Are you up for the limelight? Most people want to slide by in life, doing the minimum effort required. They live by the mentality, "How little can I do to get by?" But we've got to switch to the one-more mentality: "What's one more thing I can do to connect with this person?" Whatever they need, how can you rise to the challenge?

When you rise to the challenge of respect for others—being aware, being intentional, and executing at a high level—this will place you in the forefront of leadership. You will get noticed. For better or for worse, you won't be able to slide under the radar. You will get called on. You will get invited into the room. Are you ready? Because once you're in the room, who you are determines how long you get to stay.

Reflection Questions

1. How intentional are you about saying hello to someone when they walk into the room? Do you send the follow-up email? Do you connect with professors outside of class?
2. How can you live in the "one-more" mentality? What's one more thing you can do today to be aware and intentional in meeting someone else's needs?

CHAPTER 3

M > B

CHARACTER

WITH CLEMSON HEAD FOOTBALL COACH, DABO SWINNEY

Dabo Swinney: *Winning championships is never the top priority. When I started coaching at Clemson University back in 2009, I walked into my first staff meeting with a vision of what I wanted for each of our players. As the new head coach, I knew everyone was looking to me, waiting to see what direction I would take the team. I knew I had to set the vision early. Moreover, I had to create buy-in from each staff member so that they could internalize the vision as their own. Since that first meeting over ten years ago, our vision has remained unchanged. Here's what I want for each of our players:*

1. Graduation. *I was the first in my family to earn a college degree, and I watched that degree open doors. A diploma sets you up for life. Even though I had* *played college football, I could never have risen to head coach without that degree. I want the same doors opened for each of our players.*

2. Tools for Life. *After college, most players will pursue career paths other than football. Because most of them will head different directions, we want to equip them to succeed not only in football but in their chosen field. To do so, we created PAW Journey, a leadership program to holistically develop our players in all areas of life. Although football is important, I want them to leave Clemson with more life tools than just being a good football player. I want them to succeed in every area.*

3. Environment. *I want to create an environment where each player has a great college experience. I want them to have fun and enjoy their time at Clemson. When they play their last game and take off their cleats for the last time, I want them to look back and be able to say they had a great college experience surrounded by great people.*

4. Win a Championship. *I want each player to win a championship during their time at Clemson.*

The championships come last on the list for a reason.

I told my staff that first day, "If we succeed with the first three goals, the championships will take care of themselves." Now, over a decade later, the vision has proved true. Since 2009, every signing class has won at least one championship, some more. But we never placed championships above the other three goals. Championships simply came as we followed the greater priorities.

During my first year as an interim coach, we played a game one week, and then the next week was open. So on Tuesday of the open week, I told the team, "We're not going to have practice today. Instead, we're going to spend that time at the Children's Hospital. We're going to practice, but in a different way. We're going to practice serving the community." I caught all kinds of grief for canceling practice. But my theory paid off. By taking the time to invest in our players' character traits, we have seen them become great men, both on and off the field.

I've always said my purpose in life is simple—to glorify God in all that I do, to be a good husband and father, and to use the game of football to build great men. At Clemson, we build great men by focusing on character. Great character translates into great players, but the focus always falls on character. Winning never takes precedence. Talent can take you to the top, but only character can keep you there.

Coach Swinney's commitment to character drew me to Clemson University before I even met him. As a senior in high school, I received offers to play for major universities with competitive football programs. I won't name names, but some other universities offered monetary benefits in exchange for signing with them, which was against NCAA rules at the time. I kept going back and forth among options, struggling to decide where to go. Everyone seemed to have an opinion, trying to sway me one way or the other. However, I found an unbiased guide in my anatomy and physiology teacher, Mr. Pete Musso. He helped me weigh the pros and cons and make a decision. Finally, I decided to accept Clemson's offer. I called Coach Swinney to accept.

"I'm sorry, but right now we're full," he told me. "We can't even offer you a scholarship." He explained that I had waited too long, and they had filled all their spots. They had waited patiently for my decision but couldn't keep waiting indefinitely. They had moved on.

That rejection taught me the recruiting process wasn't all about me. It didn't matter that I was an All-American and top-ranked player in the country. Here other universities were bending the rules to get me on their team, yet Coach Swinney acted with absolute integrity. I had missed my chance, and I would have to wait my turn just like everybody else. My stats couldn't bend his character.

I waited, and thankfully a spot opened up. Clemson offered me a spot on the team the day before signing day. I had committed to another university, so I had to de-commit from them before signing with Clemson.

I had already wanted to go to Clemson, but seeing Coach Swinney's integrity reinforced my confidence I had made the right decision. He was the kind of coach I wanted to walk with. If he could walk in integrity, then I could too. If he could stand strong under pressure, then so could I.

Character attracts quality. If you want the best people on your team—whether on the field, in the workplace, or wherever you find yourself

—then hold true to integrity. Sometimes, people think they can bend the rules to get what they want—bribe here, a little sweetening of the deal there. And sometimes in the short-term, they can succeed with that method. But if you want to attract the best people and maintain long-term success, stick to character. Those with equal character will be drawn to you.

When those other universities tried to attract me by bending the rules, they actually pushed me farther away.

Investing in Players

Clemson invests in the character of players. Through daily meetings, videos, guest speakers —you name it—day by day, time after time, Coach Swinney made sure that as we played football for Clemson, we were growing a vision of who we wanted to be for life. Little did I know how much I was going to need that vision.

Clemson has a leadership program called PAW Journey, an acronym for "Passionate About Winning." The program gives players the opportunity to serve the community, receive life guidance, and prepare for their future careers after football.

When I came to Clemson as a freshman, the program didn't exist yet, but the DNA that created it was already in place. Coach Swinney and the staff at Clemson taught us to put ourselves in others' shoes by serving. The football team went to Haiti and built homes for people in need. While there, we literally washed people's feet as a symbol of how we were there to serve them. At Clemson, we hosted a shoe giveaway every Christmas for local underprivileged kids. The kids would come to pick up their new pair of shoes, and we players would kneel down to put the new shoes on for them. Over and over, Coach Swinney taught us to have a posture of serving.

He and the rest of the staff instilled in us the importance of respecting those who served us, from the cafeteria workers cooking our meals to the drivers busing us across the country. These people all devoted their time to serving us, and we sought to honor them in return. When we traveled for games, Coach Swinney made sure we cleaned the bus before we got off. When we played at away games, we left the locker room cleaner than we found it. He always told us, "How you do anything is how you do everything.

If you get the little things right, you'll get the big things right too."

He and the other staff members exemplified servant leadership. If we flew somewhere on a chartered plane, when we landed and the team boarded the bus, Coach Swinney, the president, the assistant director, and all the support staff would load our luggage for us. Like my older brother, they taught character by leading by example. They never asked us to do anything they didn't also do themselves.

Through PAW Journey, they set up a program for football players based on three pillars: Community Service, Professional Development, and Life Skills. Through professional development, they connected us with mentorship and opportunities in the business world. I interned every spring and summer for Trey Mills as a law intern. I met Billy Milam and Joe Gasque, business leaders from whom you'll hear later in the book.

By seeing us as holistic people and caring not just about our talent but our character, the staff at Clemson created the bedrock for our career through character. But I didn't realize as a freshman that in order for rock to be turned into diamond, it needs pressure. Clemson couldn't do that last step. Only God could provide the pressure truly necessary to build my character. But God promises that as he brings the pressure, he will walk with us through it. He says, "When you pass through the waters, I will be with you; and when you pass through the rivers, they will not sweep over you" (Isaiah 43:2). That was about to happen to me.

Learning to Serve

That day I left the gas station and headed onto the highway, rain pelting down on my windows, the accident changed everything. At twenty years old, all the stars aligned for me to go to the NFL. I just needed to get by for a certain period of time until it was *my* time. Clemson University was known for putting a handful of defensive linemen into the NFL draft annually. That meant all I had to do was stay in position and not get out of line.

Well, on June 3, 2017, when two thousand pounds came crashing down on me and broke my neck, the accident shifted my whole perspective on life. As the car tumbled into the ditch, my career plans tumbled with it. I received a concussion and broke three vertebrae in my neck. That particular day, God spoke to me as clear as day in that hospital bed. I lay there immobile, with tubes in every hole in my body, and I watched the oxygenated blood enter and then leave my body.

I thought to myself, "What would Jesus do?"

The answer was this: The will of his father. He would do the will of his father so that he might live more abundantly. I realized I had not been living according to his will.

How could I fix that? How could I change? It took time, just as all things do. I had to sit in God's waiting room while I waited to hear what the doctors had to say. Notice, I say "God's waiting room." The accident came from him, and I was now on his track for my life.

After a while, the doctors came rushing in to deliver the news.

"Mr. Yeargin," one doctor said, "we want to let you know that firstly, most people who do not have your stature would have died in that accident due to not having the physical strength to sustain such a crush. And second, you won't be able to play football for the foreseeable future. Instead, we are going to keep you on paralysis watch and limit all movement for the next three months.

However, as I continued to lie there, I began to feel this cool breeze and refreshment running from the top of my head down to my feet. Later I read Psalm 133:

"How good and pleasant it is
when God's people live together in unity!
It is like precious oil poured on the head,
running down on the beard,
running down on Aaron's beard,
down on the collar of his robe.
It is as if the dew of Hermon
were falling on Mount Zion.
For there the Lord bestows his blessing,
even life forevermore."

It was as if God were giving me the oil of refreshment and asking me, "What are you going to do with your oil?"

The hospital kept me on paralysis watch all that next week. Amazingly, I never became paralyzed, but I had to stay on bed rest the next two and a half months. Every movement brought pain.

Lying in bed in a neck brace for months gave me a lot of time to think. I remembered the story I learned back in Sunday School about King

David. He first became famous by battling Goliath. While he was a shepherd boy, he served in King Saul's palace. He started going out and fighting regularly, winning victories for the army, and eventually becoming the new king. He was the hero, and everyone praised him. But there's another character in the story. David had a sidekick, Jonathan.

Jonathan was the prince—the son of King Saul—and the rightful heir to the throne. When Jonathan saw God changing his life direction by choosing another man to be king instead of him, he could have felt threatened by David's rise to power. But Jonathan knew God had chosen David to be king. So instead of resenting David's position, Jonathan gave his life to serve David. They became the best of friends. When Saul threatened to kill David, Jonathan protected David and stood up for him.

Lying in that hospital bed, I realized I had always wanted to be David. I had wanted to be the hero winning all the battles. I wanted to be the man everyone praised. But I saw that if I kept trying to be David, I would miss my opportunity to be Jonathan. Instead of seeking to be the hero, I could become the servant. While my dreams of stardom only benefited myself, every person around me would benefit if I chose to serve them. I decided I wanted to be Jonathan for my teammates. For my coaches. For everyone I met.

As I lay in bed looking up at the ceiling, I told God, "I promise I will serve you with all my heart. I give every part of my life back over to you. I'll do whatever you want and go wherever you want. I'm willing to serve and be Jonathan."

That attitude shift sustained me through the hard times as I watched my NFL dreams disappear. I could be Jonathan.

Performance Versus Character

We live in a performance-based world. We can easily buy into the lie that if we perform at a high level, we can get by without developing character. But Coach Swinney taught us you won't ever be your greatest as a player until you can be your greatest as a man. Listening to Coach Swinney's inspirational speeches day after day about character, I never dreamed how much I would need them. I didn't realize it at the time, but they gave me the fuel I needed for life.

Most of the world values you based on your performance. When you perform at a high level, the world sees you as a high-value person. I saw myself through that lens. But losing my ability to perform taught me I had to base my value in something deeper. Life isn't about how you perform; it's about who you are on the inside.

I remember one time flying with Coach Swinney and two other teammates—Hunter Renfrow and Milan Richard. The four of us sat on a private flight headed to the State House as part of the tour after winning the national championship. During that flight, I was particularly struck by Coach Swinney's humility. He talked to us about why he was so thankful to serve as head coach for Clemson. He shared with us his process of getting there. He didn't focus on going down and celebrating the championship, but he focused on how thankful he was for the journey getting there, for the chance to represent Clemson, and for the privilege of sharing that moment with us. He quoted Romans 12:2, "Do not conform to the pattern of this world, but be transformed by the renewing of your mind." Just because the world measures you by your performance doesn't mean you need to live by that same standard. Instead of giving in to their system, you can rise above it. You can renew your mind by realizing the inner man matters more than the outer man. Who you are matters far more than how many games you can win or how many brand deals you can land. Your man is greater than your brand.

Instead, focus on the development of your internal gifts, and in return, they will make room for you to do more than you can ask, think, or even imagine.

Reflection Questions

1. In what areas of your life do you feel pressure to measure yourself based on your performance? How can you shift your focus in those areas to your character?
2. Who needs you to be a "Jonathan" for them? How can you spend time serving those around you?

PART II

THE MAN

CHAPTER 4
RESPONSIBILITY
WITH CLEMSON HEAD FOOTBALL COACH, DABO SWINNEY

Dabo Swinney: *At Clemson, we have a quote posted on the wall of our football team meeting room: "Right is right even if no one is doing it; wrong is wrong even if everyone is doing it." As head coach, I aim first and foremost to build great men. In order to build great men, we first must help them to think correctly. This means helping them take ownership of every part of their lives. I want them to both learn from others' mistakes and grow from their own mistakes. No matter what happens, I want them to be able to move forward in choosing to do what's right.*

We all learn by experience. That's just human nature. If a kid touches a hot stove and gets burned, he learns right away not to touch the stove again.

Pain is a great teacher. But even better is the kid who can listen to his mom tell him, "If you touch the hot stove, you'll get burned," who takes note and avoids touching it. That kid walks in wisdom. Wise people learn from others' successes and failures. They listen to others' advice and don't have to make mistakes themselves. I encourage students to always have an attitude of learning and curiosity. Explore the world, yes, but also learn from those who have gone ahead of you. Look for people who have already arrived where you want to go, and then copy the steps they took to get there.

Wisdom, however, cannot keep us from pain. You are going to have pain in your life. There's no way around it. But you can choose which kind of pain you want. You can either have the pain of self-discipline or you can have the pain of regret. Either route, you will experience pain. But I'll tell you right now—the pain of self-discipline is far better than the pain of regret.

In general, the pain of self-discipline is best. However, no one is perfect. We all make mistakes. Clemson football players come in as freshmen straight out of high school. Most of them are just now living on their own for the first time, free to make decisions without the watchful eye of their parents. I know they won't make the right decision 100 percent of the time. The key is, how will they respond when they make a mistake?

I tell my players, "If you mess up, I want to hear about it from you before I find out from someone else." This policy encourages them to own their mistakes, be honest about what happened, and learn from it. I don't expect perfection, but I do expect ownership. I want them to learn to take responsibility for their life by owning their mistakes.

We all mess up. But someone who makes a poor decision, or even faces an adverse situation over which they have no control, will let that situation define them for the rest of their life. Some will even let it destroy them. They'll look at a mistake and say, "This is what happened to me, so it must be who I am." They take on whatever identity the mishap gives them, whether it's the college dropout, the drug addict, the failed parent, the divorced spouse, and so on. From then on, the event destroys them and their quality of life. They give up on improving their life and start living under that circumstance as if they have no hope.

I want my players to see that life offers them a third option. Mistakes can define you, they can destroy you—or they can develop you. You can look at your mistake and own it. Whether the situation was your fault or not, you can look it square in the eye and say, "It happened. I can't go back in time. So how do I learn from it? How do I own it and make it right?" Every adversity brings with it an opportunity to learn and grow. But you can only grow from it if you take responsibility for the steps you take afterward.

My freshman year, after our team won the Orange Bowl, my teammate Tre and I hit the town celebrating. We broke three cardinal rules: We stayed out past the midnight curfew, we drank underage, and we had alcohol in our car. As we drove through campus, an on-campus officer pulled us over. But I took ownership in that situation. I chose to comply, and I agreed with him that we were in the wrong. We weren't taken to jail, but the event still went on our record as an arrest.

The next morning, I woke up panicked.

"What if this breaks out in the news?" I wondered. I knew I had to tell Coach Swinney, but I decided to first call Jeff Davis–the founder of PAW Journey–to get guidance before going into Coach's office.

"Look," Jeff told me. "Coach Swinney's not going to be the kind of person you think he is. Just go in, face him like a man, and tell him straight on."

So that's what I did. I walked into the office and headed straight to Coach Swinney's office. I tapped on the door. "Coach, I need to talk to you," I said. "Tre and I were out last night. We broke all the rules, but I'm going to make it right. I'm going to figure this out." I told him what we had done, and we talked about my options.

"From here on, you can make a choice to do the right thing," Coach Swinney said. "You don't have to be a product of your environment. You can clean this up and choose how you want to move forward."

In order to get the incident expunged from my record, I joined Alcoholics Anonymous and completed community service hours, volunteering in a boy's shelter and in a thrift store, and helping with Mothers Against Drunk Driving. I spent that spring semester getting help with my problem with alcohol and learning better ways to live. I took that situation as an instance where I touched the stove and got burned. I could learn not to do it again.

Tre and I both matured from that incident freshman year. Our senior year, after my car wreck, he stood up in a team meeting and called me out as a great teammate, a great brother, and someone who still cared for everyone, despite what I had been through. We both never would have been able to experience that transformation from freshman to senior year if it weren't for Coach Swinney teaching us to own our mistakes and move forward, letting them develop us into who we wanted to become.

Becoming a Father

If freshman year was the warmup, fatherhood was the real game. As a young boy, I took for granted how much I benefited from having a father in my life and seeing him serve our family day in and day out. A mother can do all she can by herself, but only a father figure can teach a boy the meaning of manhood.

I remember the day like it was yesterday. A warm spring evening in May, I got caught up in the intimacy of the moment with my girlfriend, with no thought to where my actions would lead. Fast forward two weeks later, and I thought she had food poisoning. Why else would she feel this sick? A few days later, we both knew this was more than food poisoning. I drove to the store and bought the test. We already knew the answer, but I needed those two little lines to confirm it.

My initial thoughts flew everywhere: "Are you serious? Is this test accurate? Is the baby mine? What do I do now?" And every man's favorite line, "I'm not ready to commit."

Kayla would not tolerate me riding the fence.

"Are you in or are you out?" she asked.

I had to decide.

As a man, it's hard for me to admit my fear of commitment. We act macho and tough, but the truth is, when a man is asked to fully commit his time, finances, energy, heart, and soul into raising a child—that's what separates a daddy from a father. You'll notice women use the phrase "baby daddy" when talking about the man who left them alone to raise their child. You'll never hear them refer to the "father of the child" because that title has to be earned.

All my life, I had maintained a laser focus on football, but I had been lukewarm when it came to women, finances, and life choices. I didn't consider what would happen if I kept living life so recklessly. I figured, "Plan B can fix it." Dead wrong about that one.

Now I faced the most important decision of my life: Would I commit? Could I exert that same energy I had put into creating a life and now turn it toward nurturing that new life? and realizing life wasn't about myself anymore? My son had never asked me to create him. That was my choice on my own merit.

The most important action a man can take is to commit to something. That commitment entails making sacrifices, losing sleep, doing more work than he ever expected, and—most of all—leaning on God.

Months passed by, and emotions between Kayla and me went haywire as Elijah got ready to make his grand entrance into this sinful world. I kept thinking, "Can I really do this at age twenty-two?" I had no job. I was broke. I was in graduate school. I had retired from football (I'll explain this transition more in the following chapters). My neck was still messed up from the car wreck, and I was trying to heal from surgery—a surgery I had to pay for out of pocket.

I had every excuse not to commit.

I debated what to do. At the same time, I was still walking around in a neck brace. People would ask me, "How are you doing?" and I would reply, "I'm hanging in there."

The truth was, I was on painkillers, and as a reaction to the medication, I had started having suicidal thoughts.

One particular day, I don't know if I took too much medication or not enough, but I wasn't well mentally. I went and grabbed all my painkillers, intending to overdose. But then, thank God, I chose to do what I had always done when I found myself on the brink of disaster—I called the person who had given up his life to raise me when my life threatened to careen off the rails in eighth grade. I called the person who had stood by my side after the wreck and spoon-fed me in a hospital room when I couldn't feed myself. I called my brother.

"Are you serious right now?" he said after hearing my situation.

"I'm really at that point, man," I told him. "I don't want to be here anymore. I'm frustrated. Life isn't fair. I feel like God abandoned me."

"Bro, you are selfish as hell," he replied. My brother has never been one to sugarcoat the truth, no matter the circumstances. He continued, "You are literally the most selfish person I know. After all the things you've been blessed with, you would do that to yourself? And to your son? You would leave your son here without a father, and leave Kayla to explain that to him? You have to realize life is bigger than you. It's not about you anymore. It's about your son coming into this world after you." He talked me off the edge by delivering a hard dose of reality, and he ended his plea for my life with, "If you do this right now, you might as well just light on fire everything you've ever accomplished."

I needed that verbal punch in the gut. His words might have sounded harsh, but they woke me up to the ramifications of my decision. I went to my bathroom, took a hard look at myself in the mirror, and thought, "You know what? He's right. I am selfish. Life isn't about me and what I'm going through. It's about how God is trying to use me. It's about what someone else is going through."

I had been feeling like I had nothing to give Elijah. But I realized I could give him the one thing he needed most—unconditional love. Just as Jesus Christ would give. All the other worries consuming my mind had no business distracting me from what mattered most.

I still felt fear. I was still broken. I knew that wouldn't change overnight. I knew I would have to commit to Kayla. I chose to bypass every fear that would normally deter a man from handling the responsibility in front of him. All my life, my brother and father had instilled in me, "Don't let another man take care of your responsibility." If those words didn't apply now, when would they ever? I decided I would rather break my neck again than watch my son call another man his father.

The answer was as simple as that.

No multiple choice. Just a black-and-white, fill-in-the-blank, "You are his father."

Today, Kayla and I are happily married. Kayla used to say that she knows that I didn't just marry her because we got pregnant. On our first vacation together as a couple I took her to my hometown in Florida where together we looked at wedding rings. Little did we know, she was already two weeks pregnant with Elijah. I say that to say the intention to do things in order was there, just bad timing. Today, Elijah is four years old, and our daughter, Madison, is one year old.

My mission is to make sure Elijah and Madison have everything they need from their father. Not just a monthly check, or a direct deposit into a bank account for child support, but love and guidance.

> I realized I could give him the one thing he needed most—unconditional love.

As we step up to handle our responsibilities, God is with us. God knew what I needed. He knew I needed to be tested. Every test reveals what we are truly made of. I chose to bring life into the world. Now I had to choose to take responsibility for my decisions. It wasn't too late. I still had the power to choose what was right. That choice is a gift God blesses us with.

Elijah arrived into the world at 1:44 a.m. on February 6, 2019. I knew life would never be the same. That little bundle of joy broke me down to my core. I had no idea what I had signed up for.

Reflection Questions

1. Describe a time when you watched someone else make a mistake. What did you learn from watching their experience?
2. What life circumstance has been weighing you down recently? How can you let this adversity develop you? What will it look like to make the right choice moving forward?

CHAPTER 5

TRUST

WITH CEO OF EMPLOYBRIDGE, BILLY MILAM

Billy Milam: *I first met Richard on the sidelines during a Clemson football practice. I had joined the board for PAW Journey (at that time called Fifth Quarter program). The program founder and director, Jeff Davis, invited me to come to a practice with him. Richard was clearly injured but still involved with coaching the players. At the time, I was with RaceTrac, a large convenience store chain. Richard had interviewed for an internship with them, and he knew I would be at practice that day. He came full of questions for me—not just about the business, but about life. I remember being so struck by Richard's maturity, by the complexity of his questions, and by how he had prepared for the interview. Richard had other internship opportunities, but he chose to work* *for RaceTrac, and that internship marked the beginnings of our friendship.*

Today, I count Richard as one of my closest friends, and I'm honored he asked me to share about trust. Trust is built through vulnerability, candor, and support; and if you have those elements in place, you can accomplish far more than you ever thought possible.

Building Trust

Trust comes first through our ability to be vulnerable. I've served in presidential or CEO roles the past nine years with three different companies. People call me all the time, expecting me to have answers. Sometimes I have a solution; sometimes I don't. As the leader, those times when I'm stumped require vulnerability for me to admit I don't have all the answers. I've learned I need to listen to people from every level—from the store associate to the person cleaning the coffee counter. I ask their opinions, listen to their advice, and take action based on what they say. The whole process takes vulnerability. In doing so, I build trust. The people in each company know I care about what they think. I approach each problem knowing that I might not have the answer, but between the two of us—or five of us or ten—we can find the best solution.

The second step to building trust, I borrow from the title of Kim Scott's book, Radical Candor. *I live by the principle Scott shares of being radically candid. Many people avoid tough conversations. If a problem arises, either they say nothing about the issue or they focus on the good but avoid calling out ways people can grow. But trust requires full honesty. For example, which is more effective? To say to a coworker after a presentation, "You did a great job on that presentation the other day," or to say to them, "You did a great job, but here's how I think you could land it differently next time in a way that plays more to your strengths." The second response will help your teammate grow and increase their level of trust.*

The third step to building trust is to support each other in their goals. When people see you have their back, they let down their guard and realize they can depend on you. It takes a deep level of trust to start depending on people. When I lead a team, on Day One I sit down with them and ask each person, "What is one aspect personally and one aspect professionally you would like to improve on?" Their answers will include goals like, "I need to get my numbers up," or, "I need to get better at public speaking." Then each month, the team will revisit those goals. But instead of asking each person how they're doing at meeting the goals, I'll ask the other team members, "What have you done to help this person meet their goals?" This practice creates a dynamic of team members supporting each other. When you hold each other up and learn to meet the goals together as a team, you create safety, unity, and camaraderie. When you have that level of trust on a team, you can accomplish anything.

The Impact of Trust

About fifteen years ago, during my time with RaceTrac, I received one of my first opportunities to lead a cross-functional team. The team consisted of people from real estate, engineering, construction, and store design all under one umbrella. To develop team cohesion, I started doing the practices outlined above to develop vulnerability, candor, and support. My methods were rough around the edges in those early days, but still, the team grew close.

Shortly after I had assumed leadership of the team, the board told us they wanted to build sixty new stores that year. Up until that point, RaceTrac had never built more than forty stores in one year.

"Can you do it?" they asked us.

"If the stars align perfectly, we might have a shot," I told them, "but realistically, I don't think we can pull that off."

"Well, just do everything you can to meet the goal," they replied.

So my team got to work. We started writing down everything we needed to accomplish in order to meet the goal. We worked our way backward from the end goal, then wrote down what we would need to do each month, each week, and each day to achieve the goal.

Now, here's where trust came in: We didn't sit around and wait for each person to accomplish their individual tasks. The team was so trusting and supportive that if one person fell short, another person stepped in. If Bob from real estate didn't get enough new sites under contract, Susie from construction jumped in and helped. By December 31, we had opened sixty-three new stores—three more than our "impossible" goal. That year became the first of many where I saw how trust impacted our team.

Trusting relationships have also impacted me person-

ally. As I open up in vulnerability, show candor, and offer support to friends, the guidance from those relationships has shaped the life I have today. For example, when Richard's doctor cleared him to return to football, he already had two other job offers from the corporate world, and he debated whether to accept one of those jobs or go to Boston College to start playing football again. He had recovered from his car wreck, from a torn labrum, and from spinal surgery, and no medical risks existed for returning to football. He was flying home from visiting Boston when I happened to text him to check in. He told me the situation and asked what I thought he should do.

"The way I see it, you've got a couple layups in front of you," I told Richard. "Taking one of these corporate jobs would be an easy layup. You'll be able to make the shot, no sweat, whether it's today, tomorrow, or five years from now. But playing football for Boston College will be a three-point shot. It'll take focus. It's a risk. But it's an opportunity you'll probably never get again. You might throw an airball or you might swish it in, but either way, you've got to try."

Richard accepted the offer and joined the Boston College defensive line. Not long afterward, I found myself in Boston for a job interview. I told Richard I was in town, and we met for dinner. At that point, I had worked for RaceTrac for almost twenty-two years, and I was ready for a change. I told Richard I was in Boston interviewing for a lead role with another convenience store chain. But I also had an opportunity to potentially lead a staffing company called Hire Dynamics. I worried about switching industries and thought maybe I should stay with what was familiar to me. That's when Richard turned my own advice back on me.

"I'm freezing up here in Boston because you told me to take the three-point shot," Richard said. "Sounds to me like you've got a couple layups in front of you. Whether you stay at RaceTrac or join the other convenience store chain, you could do either of those jobs easily. But the staffing company? It's new. You're scared of it. That's your three-point shot. You've got to take it."

That night, I reflected on his advice during the flight home. "He's right," I thought. "If I'm going to tell people to take the three-point shot and get uncomfortable, I've got to listen when they tell me to do the same."

Trust pushes us farther than we ever dreamed. When

we're vulnerable and candid with people, they can give us the same in return, and we can both achieve more than we ever thought possible.

To illustrate trust, I want to share the story of two friends I trusted deeply. The first friend, we'll call "Stephen." Stephen lived two houses down from me, and we grew up together. We ran with the same neighborhood mob of boys—my brother with the older boys, and Stephen and me in the younger crowd. All of us kids played outside together day and night. We played Red Light Green Light and tackle football in the grass or on the concrete. We'd ride our bikes together (or steal bikes if we didn't have any) to the corner store and buy a pack of Now and Later candy. We spent the night at each other's houses.

We ran as a pack, but Stephen and I grew particularly close. He lived next to me, and we were a team. He lived in a single-parent household. He didn't know his biological father, and his mom worked long shifts as a nurse. He lived much of his life either alone or with his stepfather.

One time Stephen and I were playing at another kid's house; we'll call him "Dougy." His mother was a police officer. When Dougy left the room, Stephen whispered to me, "I'm going to steal his game."

"Cool," I said. What did I care?

He stole it, and we left.

I went back to my house, and the next thing I knew, Dougy's mom showed up at my house.

"Where is Dougy's game?" she asked.

"I don't know," I lied. Of course I knew Stephen had it, but I had to cover for my friend, right? We did that kind of stuff all the time.

Then one night Stephen slept over at my house. We stayed up late playing, and when I woke up, Stephen had already left. He snuck out early without saying a word.

"Man, that's crazy," I thought. Then I started looking for my game. I couldn't find it anywhere. The only person who could have it was Stephen. But a lot of people came and went from our house. Surely one of them had taken it.

"Dad, I can't find my game!" I called out.

"Who was the last person over here last night?"

"Stephen."

"Then he's the one who took it."

I walked down to Stephen's house trying to pretend nothing was wrong. "Hey, bro, what's up?" I said casually.

"Nothing," he answered.

"You wouldn't have happened to have seen my game, would you?"

Stephen got quiet. I waited. Finally, he answered, "I didn't had seen it."

Okay, first he got quiet and now he couldn't even form a proper sentence? *I didn't had seen it.* What, did he have amnesia? We went outside and played like normal, but the whole time I knew he was lying to me.

"Dad," I said later that night, "I think you're right. Stephen stole my game."

"Never trust anybody," my dad replied. "You don't have friends in this world. Either they're family or they're nothing. You need to go to Stephen and tell him you know he has your game."

The next day when I saw Stephen, I was so angry I struck him, without even saying anything to him. Next thing I knew, he was on top of me beating me. We had fought before when the older boys egged us on, but this was different. We weren't scrapping just for fun; our friendship was through. He won the fight, and I never got my game back.

We didn't talk after that day.

Freshman year of high school, my family transferred me to a private school, but I still saw Stephen on our street every now and then. Whenever we saw each other, he would cross to the other side and walk by without saying a word. And I was fine with that. Our friendship was over. The next few years, he went in and out of juvenile detention. Then one day I came home from practice my senior year of high school and found police cars blocking off our street, sirens flashing. As I walked to my house, I saw that yellow tape lined Stephen's yard. Stephen had been brutally murdered. They found him dead on his bathroom floor with a note and four bullets in his head, killed by someone he had trusted enough to let inside his home.

I wished I could have paid homage to Stephen as a brother I loved and trusted. I wished we could have worked things out prior to his passing. But there was nothing to gain from talking to a person like him. He was angry over a lot of things in life that hadn't gone his way. And he had chosen his path. What he did to me, he kept doing to others. Eventually, they had gotten him back in blood.

God allowed my game to get stolen. That small betrayal protected me from continuing down the same path as Stephen. I forgive him, and now I see that God had a different route for me, one with a detour.

Be a Jonathan

At the private school, I played football with a boy named Kaylan Striggles. He lived near me and we rode the bus to school together every day. Like Stephen, Kaylan also had a single mom who worked long hours as a nurse, so after practice, my dad would pick up both Kaylan and me and drive us home. We did everything together —football, basketball, Amateur Athletic Union club. Kaylan could make anyone laugh. He played instruments, sang at his church, and evangelized to all his friends. I had finally found a friend with the same morals, someone whom I could really trust. He was Jonathan to my David.

He worked out with my brother and me and traveled with us on college visits. But we had different approaches to football. For me, life was football or nothing. On the other hand, Kaylan felt content just to take life as it came and enjoy the moment. Senior year of high school, I signed with Clemson. He went to a junior college out in California. We grew distant over the years, but he stayed loyal as the friend who supported me. When I was a no-name player in high school, he was in my corner every day. Later after my injury in college, when I was drugged out on painkillers, coke, weed, and alcohol to numb the pain, I always called him and he would make me laugh. He always answered, day or night. Eventually, he flew down to Fort Lauderdale just to support me while I checked into rehab. He was there with my brother to drop me off, and he came back at the end to pick me up. I always thought of him as the friend who supported me, but I never considered how he needed the same support.

Then one day he called me while I was at Boston College.

"Bro, I have something I need to get off my chest," he said. "You haven't been a good brother and you haven't been a good friend. And I would not be a good friend if I never called you all these years to tell you how I truly felt about you: You are selfish. I know our lives went down separate paths, but you could have at least checked in with me. You've had your successes over the years, and you've invited other people to share that with you, but you didn't think of inviting me. Even though I haven't accomplished the same things as you, my successes matter just as much as yours. You think our relationship can just continue automatically, but it won't. You've got to start investing the same amount of energy, time, and love into me that I've put into you. You need to be more thoughtful and mindful of those around you."

Talk about radical candor. He was right. I needed to hear those words. I needed to start putting in the same amount of effort into our friendship that he had. I had viewed him as my Jonathan, but I needed to be a Jonathan back to him. After that conversation, I realized I had lived with a spirit of entitlement. I had grown up with a mom, a dad, and an older brother to show me the way. Kaylan only had his mom and his brother, and his mom was often gone as a trav-

> "I would not be a good friend if I never called you all these years to tell you how I truly felt."

eling nurse. I took my life for granted instead of being mindful of his situation.

That day, Kaylan showed vulnerability and candor in opening up with me about how hurt he was and how, if I wanted the friendship to last, I would need to change.

Prioritize Trustworthy People

Kaylan and Stephen. Two friends. Two very different paths. When trying to find a trustworthy person, what do you look for? You *can* trust someone, but how do you find that person? Look for vulnerability and honesty.

Stephen never said anything harsh to my face, but then he betrayed me. Kaylan, however, told me straight up how selfish I was and then stuck by my side for life. Stephen smooth-talked me and then stabbed me in the back. Kaylan delivered the hard truth and then always had my back, no matter what.

Kaylan and I have led different lives, but we feel like we are one and the same person. We share our love for Christ and our love for people. Our core values keep us united, no matter what.

Once you find someone who shares your values and shares your passion, someone who is vulnerable and honest with you, prioritize that person. Make time for them. Know what you're looking for, and when you find a friendship like that, put in the effort to keep the friendship strong.

Reflection Questions

1. How do you show vulnerability and candor with those around you?
2. To whom do you go for advice and support?
3. How well do you receive candor from others? How do you respond when your friends, colleagues, or family come to you and tell you how you've hurt them?

CHAPTER 6
PATIENCE
WITH CEO OF EMPLOYBRIDGE, BILLY MILAM

Billy Milam: *Many young people come to me saying they want to be where I am someday—CEO of a company. They have planned their lives perfectly, lined up their goals like rungs on a ladder: "I need to get a promotion so I can afford to buy a house. Once I buy a house, then I can get married. Once I get married, then I can have kids." They plan to climb and climb until they reach the top, and they ask me how I arrived.*

Life plans are great; don't get me wrong. Goals are good. But often we become so focused on our future that we forget the importance of being the best at our role right now, wherever we are. We have our goals we set out to accomplish, and most of us want to get there instantly. We want the new house, and we want to have purchased it yesterday. Many people are so driven and focused on their goals for the future that they end up being a lesser version of themselves in the moment.

They focus one or two years down the road and miss the life they're living right now. They strive to accumulate promotions and bonuses to earn the new car, the new house, the vacation home, not realizing their extreme impatience to reach future goals is actually keeping them from being the best leader, the best spouse, or the best parent they could have been, had they just exhibited patience. When young people come to me with starry-eyed dreams for their future, I tell them that if they focus on being the best at whatever they are doing right now, the other goals will usually take care of themselves.

You've likely heard the phrase, "Bloom where you're planted." Although cliché, it stands true. The key to a truly happy, successful life lies in having the patience to focus on your role right now. Patience allows us to slow down and focus on the most important aspects of life: serving and caring for others, regardless of what we gain from it.

Yes, set goals. But don't forget to patiently accept how

long it may take you to meet that goal. Whether you're a student, a parent, a professional, a professor, or anything in-between, look at your role today and ask, "How can I be the best at it?" Don't let your goals distract you from patiently focusing on your life right now.

Patience Is Active

A lot of people hear the word "patience" and imagine just sitting still, waiting for something to happen. But I've learned that patience is a grind. Patience requires a willingness to keep putting in the work, even when you don't see the results.

Anything we want in life takes time to achieve and requires that we follow a process. After my car wreck in 2017, I had to go through a year of physical therapy and rehabilitation. I couldn't rush the healing process. I came back to play in 2018 and soon afterward tore my labrum in a routine tackle during practice, ending my season instantly.

More months of therapy.

More time to heal.

I decided to undergo a spinal surgery to repair my neck–the same surgery that Peyton Manning had been through in 2011. After that surgery came more doctors, more appointments, and more exercise regimens as I tried to heal completely.

The grind hurt. I pursued healing with no promise of the outcome I wanted. My doctors couldn't give me any guarantee that I would ever fully heal or return to football.

While I was recovering from surgery, I leaned on drugs to get through the pain. Not just painkillers, but weed, cocaine, and alcohol. Like I mentioned in the last chapter, I started back going to rehab to break my addiction. I had to show up at rehab every day–both physically and emotionally–putting in the work necessary to restore my mental health. Again, I had to grind while I was waiting to get better.

The results took time, but eventually I began to see the fruit of my labor. In April 2019, God offered me a second chance at football. I traveled down to Florida after the death of my grandma (my mom's mom) and decided to get another medical assessment while in town, so I went back to my doctor. After running some tests, he sat down with me to review the results.

"I have something to tell you," he said with a serious face.

"Come on, man, what's it now?" I asked. "Just lay it on me."

"You can play again."

"Doc, don't mess with me like that." I could not believe it, but he was serious. I could play football again after a two-year mental, physical, and emotional battle.

I talked the decision over with Kayla and the rest of my family to see if they had any concerns. They told me that they had none, as long as I wasn't putting my health in jeopardy or risking paralysis.

I risked the three-point shot and went back to playing football.

So checkmate, right? My patience had paid off and I had received a second chance at my dreams. The work was done, right?

Not so much. Returning to football and signing on with Boston College marked the fulfillment of a longtime dream, but that season required its own dose of patience. Because of all my injuries, although I no longer risked paralysis, I still sustained some injuries early on. Soon after I arrived, I had to have my knee worked on due to old damaged cartilage from a right medial meniscus tear. I probably needed to have surgery on my labrum, but I didn't because it would cause further delay in my process of getting back active on the field. Needless to say, I was in constant pain and I couldn't practice most days, so I just played in the games. After two or three games, they placed me as a full-time starter for the team. I was in pain, but I also felt an incredible depth of gratitude for every second I got to step back onto that grass.

The injuries required patience, and so did joining an entirely new team. I knew that as the new guy on the team, I might be perceived as a potential threat. Most of the players had joined the team as freshmen and worked their way up, just as I had done at Clemson. Now here I was, a six-foot-four transfer showing up to take their spot. I had to come in with humility and patience.

On day one, I called a players' meeting with the whole defensive team to explain to them my story and vision for the team. One of the linebackers, Max Richardson, was captain of the defense. I asked him, "What are you faced with, and how can I help?" We started going through film together and brainstorming a plan for the defense. We ran the plan by Coach Addazio. Then Richardson met with his linebackers, I met with my defensive line, and we got everyone into accord. As I approached the team with an attitude of serving them, they then started turning the question around and asking what they could learn from me, since I had come from Clemson. We developed a great working relationship right from the start.

Because I started with patience, the team allowed me to bring the same mentality and work ethic I had learned at Clemson into the practice rooms of Boston College. I would stay in the weight room until one or two in the morning, helping guys with their workouts after practice. We would arrive early to watch film before practice or games. We were together all the time. Then my position coach, Coach Jim Reed, took such a liking to me that he asked me to be a captain of my segment group. I wasn't looking for that opportunity, but the whole atmosphere had shifted as we worked together, and everyone noticed my natural leadership take over. The Atlantic Coast Conference awarded me the Brian Piccolo award for being the "most courageous" player of the year. I got to share my story with

ESPN, *The Boston Globe*, *The Jim Rome Show*, ACC Network, and a plethora of other major media outlets.

I got to fulfill my dream, but at the same time, I knew my chance to play football wasn't about me. It was about inspiring others. For my jersey, I chose number 2, which stood for second chances.

Condition, Circumstances, and Conclusion

Wherever you are, know that your internal condition and your external circumstances do not determine your conclusion. I learned this concept of the three C's (Condition, Circumstances, and Conclusion) when I attended Coach Chris Crumpler's King Conference. Jeremy Anderson and Crumpler shared this teaching, and it resonated. Throughout my life, I've had times where I felt like all the cards were stacked against me and I should have failed.

I had an internal condition. The grind of going to physical therapy and moving in and out of rehab revealed to me that mentally, I wasn't in a healthy spot. I struggled with regret, addiction, anger, depression, and so many other issues.

Regarding my external circumstances, I came

from struggles growing up, including loss and death in the family. I came from a car wreck and from my dreams being taken away. As I headed to Boston College, I didn't have a clue what I was doing. I had just gotten engaged. I was a new father. I didn't have a house, and we were moving back into student housing. Deciding to become a student again meant postponing my career. I was uprooting Kayla and Elijah, expecting them to enter with me into an entirely different environment from Florida—an environment that was temporary and would soon change again.

When the conditions and circumstances felt stacked against me, I had to trust someone greater than me. I had to apply my faith. I had to shift mentally from being overwhelmed by my problems to determining to overcome them. My condition and my circumstances were not excuses to fail. They were only reasons to succeed.

It took time to develop that mindset. I had to be patient as I dealt with myself over the course of two years. I had to sit with all of the pain, all of the regret from my bad choices, all of the debt hanging over my head and realize, "I can't let these things determine my outcome."

I decided to double down and bet on myself.

My condition and my circumstances did not define my conclusion. Sure, I was injured. Mentally and physically, I wasn't as sharp after taking a break from football for two years. I had to be patient with myself as I adjusted to suddenly being thrust onto the football field again.

But my first practice at Boston College, I knelt down and touched the turf.

"Man," I thought, "I am living my wildest dream."

After years of fighting to get back on the field, I had finally made it. I knew I couldn't walk into the locker room with anything other than gratitude. I got a second chance to pursue my dream. How could I be anything but grateful?

Living in Boston felt like getting a fresh start mentally. The air was crisper, the weather colder —everything about my environment was new. My conditions and circumstances seemed to melt away. Within months, I was living a different life than I had ever imagined. I got to finish my dream of playing college football.

I learned that, at the end of the day, my success wasn't determined by my condition or my circumstances. My success was determined by how much I served others, shared my story to inspire hope in them, and trusted that God had a plan bigger than what I could imagine. I leaned on faith. When I didn't think it was possible, God gave a new conclusion and a new outcome.

Fulfill Your Destiny

Patience means staying in the grind. We can't just sit on the sidelines and hope to magically become a better player someday without putting in the work. If we want to be a good athlete, we have to hustle, we have to lift the weight, we have to get up extra early, and do the workout we don't want to do. That's how life works. The opportunities eventually come, but they only come after patience accompanied by hard work.

So many people look at the amount of work it will take to reach their goals and they get stuck. They want the result, but they don't want the grind. They think, "This will take forever; how am I ever going to reach my goal?" But here's the deal: time doesn't matter when you're doing quality work.

If you are feeling overwhelmed by a goal, just take one step. Focus on your goal one day at a time, one hour at a time, one minute at a time. When I lay in a hospital bed on paralysis watch, I couldn't think about how long it would take to recover. I had to just think about getting through the next hour. And then the next day. And then the next week. When I finally returned to football in 2018 and then injured my shoulder right away, I couldn't think about the goal of ever playing football again. I just had to focus on my next step to heal. In rehab, I couldn't think about how long I would have to be in there. I just showed up for that moment and did that day's work. And somehow, I got through it. While I was being patient, waiting for my opportunity to manifest, I kept putting in the work.

Patience means staying in the grind.

Patience is the only way you can reach your destiny and fulfill it. If you are faithful with the few things in front of you, God will entrust you with much.

Reflection Questions

1. Are you serving and caring for others, apart from what you can gain from them? Are you being the best version of yourself right now, where you are?
2. Think of a challenging situation in your life or an overwhelming goal. What is the next step you can take? How can you exhibit active patience while you're waiting for it to resolve?
3. What are you so diligently waiting for? What have you manifested internally that will reflect externally?

PART III

THE KING

CHAPTER 7
CLASS
WITH CEO OF MEDSHIFT, JOE GASQUE

Joe Gasque: I first met Richard through PAW Journey's professional program back in 2019. I was with GE Healthcare visiting Clemson for a career day. I have to say, in the four years I have known Richard, I have learned far more from him than I have taught him. However, I will share a few lessons I've learned throughout my life on how to conduct yourself with class. Having class comes down to treating people well, consistently and regardless of circumstances.

Be a great teammate, someone with whom others want to work. Show up for your team, be authentic, and treat others how you would want them to treat you. When you treat others with class, they usually start reciprocating and treat you with the same care. Bring a great attitude to work every day and be coachable. Stay open to receiving feedback and try to learn and grow from it. When you consistently work hard, have a great attitude, and have fun along the way, good things will happen to you. Granted, they might not happen in the first few months, or even in the first few years, but if you keep showing up consistently, good things will come.

Another key element to treating people with class is to trust them from the start. The more trusting you are, and the less cynical, the better you will end up treating people. You might not even be thinking about it, but people can sense whether you trust them or not.

Most people set out with the mindset that their trust has to be earned. Under this mindset, they subconsciously assign everyone an F on the trustworthiness scale. And then if people earn trust, they slowly work their way up to an A—if they earn it.

But I like to give people my trust from the start. Everyone sets out with an A, and they keep that A unless they prove to me they don't deserve it. There's a big difference between making someone earn your trust versus giving that person your trust automatically until they lose it. When you start out trusting people, this allows you to, "move at the speed of trust," as I like to call it. If I walk into a room and assume everyone is trustworthy, we can get to work. We can solve problems faster and tackle issues head-on. However, if I don't trust people, that mistrust slows down the process of working together. If I'm unwilling to depend on people or listen to them, I slow down what we could accomplish.

Start out trusting people, assuming they want the best for you just as you do for them, and you'll end up treating people with class. You'll be more open, kind, and helpful.

The third element to having class is to always treat people well, regardless of how they treat (or mistreat) you. Yes, most people will reciprocate when you treat them with class, but not everyone. We've likely all experienced office politics, whether our employees are having conflict, a colleague is manipulating a situation, or a boss is taking advantage of us. When you find yourself in those situations, how do you respond?

I encourage people to view conflict through this lens: life is short, but a career is long. In other words, you will be in the workforce for most likely for thirty to fifty years. How you treat someone today may affect your career ten or twenty years down the road. Play the long game. If your boss, client, or co-worker underappreciates your value, keep your cool and act in a way that preserves the relationship. Who knows? Thirty years later, you might be glad you did.

We've all seen that incinerating email come across the screen. You really want to prove them wrong and write a nasty email in return. You type it out but don't hit send. Then you sleep on it, maybe get a little exercise, and come back the next day only to read the draft and think, "Good thing I didn't send it." Having class saves you the pain of regret.

When you always take the high road, no matter how you feel in the moment, you'll be able to look back on your career without regret, and you'll be glad you treated everyone with kindness and respect, no matter what.

As I was going through material for this book, I came across a letter from my second-grade teacher, Miss Elizabeth. She wrote an endorsement for when I joined a mentorship program, and she shared these memories of me as a second-grader:

I remember Richard as one of my past students in second grade, who I can proudly say made me beam with pride each time I remember his amazing work attitude. He had the best penmanship ever. Not to mention he was totally confident, yet humble. His personality was noticeable the moment I came in contact with him. He has always been about continued success, and he was selfless on his mission, even when he was in second grade.

I had amazing examples of what it meant to have class—from my mother and grandmother to all of my wonderful preschool teachers at Phyl's academy, my second-grade teacher Miss Elizabeth, and my fourth-grade teacher Miss Carla. Even in second grade, I had a teacher who called out the good in me, but then by eighth grade, I had been kicked out of the pre-law program and labeled an at-risk student. As I shared in Chapter One, I left my gift behind to skip class.

Throughout my life, I have received second chance after second chance. High school was a second chance to relearn class. I attended three private schools for high school: two Catholic and one Jewish. Starting from the first day on campus at the Catholic school, I had to wear a collared shirt, khakis, and Skechers. At the next school, the dress code was taken to an even higher level, and I had to wear a suit jacket, collared shirt, vest, sweater, dress shoes, and even dress socks every single day. Simply dressing differently affected how I carried myself. I adapted to the rigorous atmosphere of discipline. The environment groomed me and taught me how to carry myself with class in the community.

Both Catholic schools required all students to attend mass. I was Baptist, but attending mass taught me to be mindful of other people's beliefs. And at the Jewish school, I gained exposure to a third religion. I learned to respect others' beliefs. We have to be truly diverse, equitable, and inclusive of those around us. Having class means being mindful of all people around you.

At the third private school my senior year, I played football under Coach Roger Harriot at University School. He and I developed the best high school coach-athlete relationship you can imagine. He was like a father to me, and the picture of class. He had five kids, and each one of them grew up to be a success. I saw how he honored his wife, made time for his family, and still somehow managed to be an excellent coach and administrator. He showed me having class meant not just treating the outside world well, but also respecting and cherishing those closest to you.

My senior year, I won the Watkins Award, which honors the nation's top five outstanding African American male high school seniors who excel both athletically and academically. Along with the award came an invitation to the White House to receive it. Receiving the Watkins Award symbolized the full realization of my second chance in high school—from leaving my gift behind to coming back and reclaiming what was mine. And now in the spring of 2023, I was invited to return to Washington, D.C., this time to induct a new class of young men receiving the award. I get to come back this time as a guide for those following behind me. To whom much is given, much is required.

I am now at a turning point in my life of starting to lead others. I serve as a professor at Clemson University and will begin work this fall on a Ph.D. in educational leadership organizational development. I've been inducted into the 5,000 Role Models program as a mentor for at-risk minority boys. The program aims to give at-risk youth mentorship and positive role models in hopes of decreasing their dropout rate and showing them a better path in life. I now mentor hundreds of young men around Broward County, many of them attending the public schools I would have gone to had I not attended private school. When I go back into those neighborhoods, I see myself. I was the at-risk male in eighth grade, and now I get to go back and pour into those young men just like so many others did for me.

Recently at church, I spotted a boy who came out of the foster care system. I am friends with his parents, and I know that after they adopted him, he still battled mental health issues and even tried to take his own life. He's only eleven years old, but his parents have decided to check him into a ninety-day program that will hopefully give him the help he needs. On Sunday, the family sat a few rows ahead of me, and as I stood in church that day watching him, I saw myself in him. I was the kid fighting on the streets, toughing it out, trying to prove myself to my peers, but then hating myself and wanting to take my own life. As I watched that boy, I started to weep for him. I know everything he'll have to endure if he wants to make it in life. I also know that boy's calling is so big—God has great plans for him, but he will have to go through struggles to reach that destiny.

Having class means so much more than just using good manners and treating people with respect. Class is about being able to place yourself in someone else's shoes, to be mindful of their situation, to honor them instead of judging them, and to recognize that you could easily be in their same situation. When you see people with compassion, you automatically start treating them with class, no matter who they are.

Taking the High Road

My parents showed me early on to conduct myself with class no matter how people treated me. Like I mentioned, I went to a private school my freshman and sophomore year. When I enrolled, I was an at-risk student, but the school gambled on me and gave my parents a discount on tuition for me to attend and play football. Their gamble paid off. I excelled both academically and athletically. I became an engaged student and football player. Then, because I did so well, I received an opportunity to transfer to a different private school–one that had a superior football program. I was playing out of position at my current school, but the new school would let me play in my preferred position as a linebacker.

I decided to transfer there for my junior year. Although the first private school had been good to me, taking a risk on me and setting me up for success, I knew that transferring to the new school would provide the best opportunities for furthering my football career.

When the first school's administration heard about my decision to transfer, things got ugly. They withheld my transcript and did other conniving moves, making it very difficult for me to leave. It was a bitter ending.

But my mom and dad had an idea. The day we went to the school to pick up my transcript and release papers, we brought in balloons and a thank-you card. My parents reminded me the school had been good to us in providing academic instruction, a partial scholarship, and athletic development that furthered my skills in football. I could display gratitude towards them, even though they treated me poorly at the very end.

We walked into the office, and nobody talked to us, not even the principal. We picked up the papers, left the balloons and thank you cards at the front desk, and walked out into the sunshine.

That moment always stuck with me. I learned that no matter how someone treats you, you can still show them kindness, even if it's on your way out. Always leave a place better than you found it. Even if people gossip about you, slander you, or otherwise mistreat you, you can still leave with class.

And God blessed my decision to leave. When I arrived at the new school, I stepped into an ideal situation. As a junior, I got to step up and be a leader on the team. They placed me as a linebacker, and that year I received my first scholarship offer—to Clemson University.

Reflection Questions

1. Joe Gasque mentioned moving "at the speed of trust." Why does trust increase efficiency? Do you usually give people their trust or wait till they earn it?
2. How can you be more mindful of those around you? How can you show empathy to those in difficult situations?
3. Think of a situation, either past or present, where you felt mistreated. How can you treat the other party with class, even when they don't deserve it?

CHAPTER 8
INTEGRITY
WITH CEO OF MEDSHIFT, JOE GASQUE

Joe Gasque: *During my first manager job at GE Healthcare, I had to execute a round of layoffs. In my twenty-five year career, those layoffs were the hardest task I ever had to complete. The nights leading up to the layoffs, I couldn't sleep. We were about to lay off great members of our team. I knew each person had a family to feed and bills to pay, and our decisions directly affected their livelihood. But we had to reduce costs by decreasing our number of employees.*

I entered each layoff conversation with the buttoned-up script from the human resources department. The script contained all the proper terminology to keep us from getting sued. But when I sat down with each employee to tell them we were ending their role with the company, their first question was always "Why?"—Why me? Why now? I knew I couldn't look them in the eye, deliver a heartless script, and still be able to look myself in the mirror when I went home that night. I had to conduct the conversations from the heart.

I walked them through the reasons why, sticking as close to the HR script as I could, but I still affirmed their value as team members and being fully truthful with them. I then followed up after the conversation, making sure they had the resources necessary to find a new role at another company. And at the end of the process, I could sleep well at night. I could go home, look myself in the mirror, and know I had done everything within my power to care for those employees.

Integrity means showing honesty, care, and respect. It starts first as a responsibility to God and then carries over into a responsibility to family and community. I had to care for my employees as people, recognizing the hardship I was placing on them and their families. I had to respect and honor them as individuals and as great team members. Even though we faced a difficult situation, I still affirmed them. I showed up in an authentic way and was truthful to them.

Foxes and Pebbles

When I think of integrity, I like to use an analogy I learned from an elder at my church: the foxes and the pebbles. Both will come at you, and you have to be ready.

When we try to live with integrity, we easily see the big temptations coming at us and know to steer clear. Like foxes, the big temptations are easy to recognize, and we know how to avoid them. For example, we know not to drop out of school. We know we should graduate. We know we need to provide for our family. We can focus on big-picture integrity and think we're doing a great job living with integrity. But it's usually not the foxes that trip us up. We see them coming and we avoid them. No, it's all the little pebbles, the things we don't even think about, that trip us up. They're smaller, so we miss them, and they actually pose a far greater danger.

For example, I don't have an issue providing for my family. But I do have an issue with delegating. I tend to take on too many commitments and end up spending too much time working, which results in the neglect of my family. I put my work before my wife, and my career becomes my mistress. I could have delegated. I could have asked someone else to do it. But instead, I did it. I can get so focused on pursuing my mission that I lose sight of the influence I have within my own home.

It's the little pebbles like this that we often overlook. We walk down life's path, not looking where we're going until we trip up and realize if we had only paid attention, we wouldn't be in this situation.

Reactive Versus Proactive Integrity

I've spent a lot of time in different forms of rehab centers. Coming off of multiple drug addictions, I've heard people talk about how you can't just tell yourself, "I won't do drugs," or, "I won't drink alcohol." You can't just focus on avoiding what's bad; you have to proactively fill your life with what's good. There needs to be a twelve-step program for integrity. You need to look at who you want to be, and then focus on what you need to do to get there.

As an inspirational public speaker, I travel around the country for different events. A few months ago, my wife and I traveled to Atlanta to attend a conference. We arrived the day before the conference started, and as we were in the hotel lobby checking in, I saw a woman off to the side working as a prostitute. She tried to signal my attention, even though I was clearly with my wife. I ignored her.

Back when my wife and I were dating in college, we used to go to Atlanta and party, but that life was behind us. I was focused on the conference and my speaking engagement, so we decided to stay in that night.

My good friend Kaylan Striggles lives in Atlanta and works as a comedian now. I wanted to prioritize seeing him while I was in town, so I invited him over to the hotel that evening. He came to see me, and we sat in the lobby chatting it up for a while. After we said our goodbyes and he left, the same young lady I mentioned earlier approached me.

"Hey, you got a wife?" she asked.

She had just seen my wife earlier that day. I was still wearing my wedding ring.

"Yes, I have a wife," I answered.

"Well, what does that matter?"

"Absolutely not," I said. "I'm good. I'm praying for you, but I've got to go." I pushed past her and got onto the elevator.

In college, that same interaction would have tripped me up. I would have made a wrong turn, given her my number, and done something conniving. But now I am at a different point in life. I am committed to God and to my wife. I live in abundance and overflow. God has given me responsibilities as king over my family, my ministry, and my career, and he calls me to rule with integrity. Integrity requires commitment to sacrifice—starving fleshly desires and not conforming to the ways of the world. The Bible says I have been crucified with Christ, and I no longer live, but Christ lives in me (Galatians 2:20). Every day, I get up early and serve God because I have already died to my flesh. Life isn't about me anymore. It was easy for me to avoid the bad because I had already filled my life with what is good.

I have spent years learning how to be faithful to Kayla, diligent in my calling, mentored by men wiser than me, part of a church community, and building my career. I work to keep God's word at the forefront of my mind, not just an afterthought. Because I have filled my life and my heart with what is good, there's no room for evil.

Integrity means not just avoiding what's wrong, but actively pursuing what is right.

The Four A's of Integrity

Whenever I speak to groups about integrity, I like to share with them the four A's: Alignment, Assignment, Adjustments, and Accountability. My defensive line coach, Marion Hobby, who now coaches for the Cincinnati Bengals, drilled this acronym into us during my time at Clemson. I can still hear him asking us, "What's your alignment? What's your assignment? You better know your adjustment."

Over the years, I've realized the four A's apply to more than just defensive strategy on the football field. They apply to integrity as well.

1. **Alignment**—Suppose you've driven your car for over five thousand miles. You take it in for a maintenance check, and what's one of the first things the mechanic does? He checks

your tires' alignment and determines whether they need to be rotated. Why? To ensure that you're able to get the maximum use out of your vehicle. Likewise, God says we must be aligned with him before we can be effective anywhere else. You have a purpose. In order to walk in integrity, you must find God's purpose for your life and align yourself with his direction. If you don't know where you're going, how will you recognize a wrong turn? But when you know your purpose and have direction, you can easily steer away from anything not in alignment with it.

2. **Assignment**—Along with your purpose comes a specific assignment. God has gifted you in certain areas. Discover how God wants to use you, and then let him. It's your job to do your due diligence in finding out how God has gifted you and then be obedient to whatever responsibilities he has given you.
3. **Adjustments**—We all start somewhere, but integrity requires us

not to stay there. We have to change and grow. Once we know our life purpose and mission, we have to look at where we currently are and realize that in order to go from point A to point B, we will need to make some changes. Rising to the challenge always requires growth. I grew from a boy into a man, but I was still a broken man. I had to make adjustments to come into alignment with God's purpose and be ready for his assignments. And then I had to move from being not just a healed man, but walking in abundance as a king.

4. **Accountability**—You can't walk in integrity on your own. No one can. We all need people around us to guide, challenge, correct, and encourage us. I have pursued surrounding myself with many mentors because I know I need them. Joe Gasque and I connect every one or two months—and then I have Jon Gordon, Jon Christiansen, Jeremy Anderson, Billy Milam, and so many

> others that I check in with regularly. Having mentors motivates me because I know that if I mess up, I won't just disappoint myself and my family, but I will also let all of them down too.

Integrity means not just avoiding what's wrong, but actively pursuing what is right.

Having the four A's in place takes time and requires work. But each A—aligning with your purpose, knowing your assignment, making adjustments in order to grow, and surrounding yourself with accountability—will allow you to be proactive in pursuing integrity. These four A's will protect you from tripping over the pebbles because you will be proactively filling your life with everything good.

Reflection Questions

1. What is your life's purpose and assignment? How can you be proactive about pursuing them?
2. What are some pebble issues that might have the potential to keep you from aligning with your purpose? How can you address them?
3. Who are people in your life who regularly hold you accountable? If you don't have anybody, how can you start those relationships?

M > B

CHAPTER 9
LOVE

WITH MY WIFE, KAYLA YEARGIN

Kayla, my Queen: *There's no complexity to it. Misery loves company. Rich and I got together while we were both in a pit and at what seemed to be rock bottom. I had hit a low point in my life. My self-esteem was demolished, college was not going as planned, and I was broken from previous relationships. Right when I had made up my mind to get my life back on track, Rich hit the scene. Interesting. Who knew that a simple direct message on Instagram would lead to the life I'm living with him now?*

Like I said, I had low self-esteem when we started dating. And like any other insecure girl in a relationship, my tolerance for mistreatment was exponentially high. My mastery at overlooking red flags only drew me closer and closer to him. It was not too deep into our relationship when I found out I was not the only component. There was more.

"But you are my main girl," he told me as if that were to make me feel better and keep me around. Well it did. I became a broken record by the amount of times I told him it was over, only to be smooth-talked back into being his "main girl." After all, I was broken. He was my only friend at the time. Where was I going to go? I could never stay mad at him for too long anyway. There was something about him that made me want to stay. He may not have been the best boyfriend. But he was truly my friend and a joy to be around while I was in my pit.

I often went back and forth with myself, saying, "You decided to get in a relationship with a Clemson football player right after they won another national championship. This kind of treatment is to be expected." From what I knew, Richard's future looked bright. And like so many other girls, my mentality should have been, ride this wave and my future would look bright too. Whether I'd be an NFL wife or a baby mother, my life would be set if I stuck it out with him. However, this was not my mentality. Was it weird that I did not want Richard to go to the NFL? I liked Richard a lot. He grew on me. I didn't want to lose him to the game. I selfishly wanted him to myself. Without the shenanigans. After all, if he was doing me wrong now at college level, how worse off would it be at the next level? God must have heard my prayer because June 3, 2017, happened. Ouch. Richard's football career seemingly vanished before our eyes. He was restricted and put on bed rest. I knew this meant no more side girls—or so I thought. I remember the day he came home from the hospital. Dressed in injuries. I was there making sure he ate and making sure he got bathed. One night he went to the bathroom and left his phone on the bed. A Facetime call came in from a girl who was not his family. I asked him who this was Facetiming him. He gave me a blank stare. Then he told me the truth. She was someone he messed around with whenever he traveled back to his hometown. She had heard the news of his accident and was wanting to book a flight to come see him. "Isn't that something?" I thought.

One night I took advantage of his state. While he was sleeping, I used his thumbprint to go through his phone. Big mistake. I was disgusted at all that I found in there. This dude had a surplus of girls in his thread all waiting for him to make it big so they could make it too. I decided to screenshot all the evidence, send it to myself, and then send it to him as a way to break up with him the next day. The next morning came. I went to work, sent him my evidence, and broke up with him via text. He showed up at my door later that day. He was supposed to be on bed rest and not supposed to operate a vehicle. He did anyway. All to explain and come clean and apologize. I remember seeing him at my front door in that lousy neck brace with sadness in his eyes. He knew he was messed up. I knew it too. But he was the one who wronged me, so why on earth did I feel sorry for him? Like I said earlier, I could not stay mad at him for long. I knew he needed me—my prayers, my love, and my patience. As he was healing from his injury, he mentioned the girls he was dealing with no longer wanted to be bothered with him now that his football career wasn't certain. I tried not to laugh at this, but it was funny to me. Here I was sticking it out with him while everyone else was falling off like dead flies. The irony.

When Richard and I found out we were pregnant a year later, fear came over both of us. As you could probably already imagine, he was not ready to be a father and I did not feel ready to be a mother. Especially not with someone who I felt was not fully committed to me. As Richard mentioned in a previous chapter, he had to make a choice. I was no longer playing games with him. Either he was in or he was out. Having a baby has a way of pulling the woman out of a girl. You all of a sudden get this boldness and move with a sense of urgency. Your tolerance for nonsense decreases as you begin to think about the future of your child. I decided to raise my child with or without Richard's help. This decision was a turning point for the both of us. For the first time, he witnessed me give him an ultimatum and mean it. And for the first time, I saw him choose me and be all in.

Being in this relationship was not at all easy. But when you invest in someone, it makes it hard to leave. Rich and I have been in the valley many times and for long periods of time. But through those valleys, I knew the seeds that I planted in our relationship would come to bear fruit one day. Think about it this way: Imagine a farmer plants seeds all season long and then completely leaves his field right before harvest season. That's stupid. The good Lord said that you shall reap what you sow, and I know what was sown in this relationship. I made a decision to stick around and reap our harvest. Writing this right now, Rich and I are definitely in a season of harvest. I look back at how far we've come, and it amazes me every time.

I just want to make this clear for any female readers: I am not at all advocating for anyone to stay and tolerate mistreatment in any relationships. This advice is for the ones who may be in relationships and who are unaware of their worth and settle a little. But I say God will give you beauty for ashes and that is what he did for me. You have to know what and whom you are dealing with. I had the ability to look past Richard's shortcomings and see into his heart. I believed with all my heart that Richard was a good person deep down. I believed that he wanted to do right. But he was just stuck in his ways. A lot of his misbehavior was a cry for help. He just wanted and needed to be loved. I could tell that he needed inner healing. Hurt people hurt people. And many don't understand why they hurt people; they just do. I pray for people like this. I was there for him even when he did not deserve it. I chose to pray for him whenever he was in the wrong. I chose to love him even though he did not always do the same for me. I was invested in the man that I knew he'd become and not his brand. Yes, on the outside he was a Clemson football player seemingly destined to go to the NFL. Most would be mesmerized by his stardom, but I wanted what was inside of him. What I invested in went deeper beyond the surface. And in the end, I got the man over the brand.

Royalty Is Earned

Two years ago, Kayla left me. This time, it wasn't a one-day break-up where we got back together later that afternoon. No, this time she was really done. We'd had a child out of wedlock, and we were shacking up but still not married. We lived with no spiritual integrity. And I was a very broken man. After finishing my time at Boston College in 2020, I then spent all my finances preparing for the NFL draft. But the COVID-19 pandemic was in full swing, making everything harder. I didn't make the draft, and I found myself bankrupt with no job. We moved back home to Florida, and I depended on my parents to support me while I continued to train for the next NFL draft. During this time, I abused Kayla physically and verbally. I was on drugs. I remember even snorting crack cocaine before picking my son up from school. Kayla would find me drugged out, and she was done. In 2021, she took our son and left.

And she was right to leave me.

I was mentally and emotionally unstable. I would go through bouts of depression and suicide ideation. An elder at church shared with me a marriage concept he had learned about the buffalo and the butterfly. As men, we can live like a buffalo, not realizing we've been partnered with a delicate butterfly. If we're not careful, we can trample her. Looking back, I realize I was living as a buffalo, and I was crushing this sweet butterfly I had been given. All my life, I had trained to be tough. The world saw the six-foot-four-inch, rocked-up, aggressive man. But they didn't see the man screaming on the inside to be loved, to be hugged. I didn't even know that was okay. I concealed my emotions, pretending everything was fine, and then I would explode on Kayla. I was stampeding at this butterfly, trying to put her in a jar and keep her, and it just wasn't working.

Her departure broke me. I had to change the way I was living. I had to get my life in order. One of my mentors I'd had since college, Jon Christiansen, invited me to live at his house in

South Carolina. He had mentored me back in college and encouraged me to pursue a master's degree. We kept in touch over the years, and when I told him everything that had happened, he invited me to come live with him.

"Look, we all make mistakes," he told me after I moved in. "We all fall short, but that doesn't mean you can excuse your behavior. So let's work on fixing it."

And then he showed me how. We developed a game plan to set my life in order. He worked with me every day, helping me set goals, check my progress, and take the next step with writing down how I was feeling each day.

With Jon's help, I realized that not being able to provide for Kayla and Elijah financially was just the beginning of ways I had failed her. I wasn't mentally stable. I wasn't present for her emotionally. I didn't listen to her. I had focused on the outer things—buying the right clothes, owning the best brands, impressing her with fancy dinners—but in focusing on the brands, I had completely neglected her. And then I had even bankrupted us financially.

Jon helped me slowly cultivate new soil. My life was filled with weeds, and he helped me root up the old patterns and then plant new seeds in new soil. He taught me to live with a new identity—to see myself as a man of character who operates out of his faith and walks in integrity, honor, and valor in everything he does. When we start seeing ourselves in a new light, we start becoming that new person.

Kayla and I didn't talk for the first few months after she left. Then I went up to visit them in Detroit where they were living with Kayla's mother, and we met with our pastor.

In counseling, he told us, "You don't have to like each other. You don't even have to get along with each other. But you *will* respect each other as the parents of your children."

That conversation was the turning point for us. We committed to respecting each other even if we couldn't get along.

The following months, I traveled back and forth between South Carolina and Michigan to visit Elijah. During that time, Kayla and I started seeing each other with new eyes. All the past hurts and offenses started to fade away.

One day we went together to Jon's sister Tam, a chiropractor, to get adjusted and—I kid you not—Kayla and I came out of that appointment in total alignment with each other, fist pumps and everything. The stress and worries of life fell off for just a moment, and we were back on the same team. I felt that day that if I could just play the long game, we would eventually get back together.

During our recovery season, I realized that as much as I needed to pour into Kayla, I also needed to pour into her mother. Not only had I hurt Kayla, but my behavior had hurt her family too. Her mother had entrusted me to care for her daughter, and I had let both of them down. I continued to show up in the relationships, to make adjustments to my behavior, and to live in accountability with Jon and others. This buffalo was slowly learning how to earn the trust of a butterfly.

Kayla and I got married on March 16, 2022.

The Seeds of Love

When people think of love, they usually think of romance and passion. Yes, love includes those elements. But love is more so about brokenness, forgiveness, and faith in God. I have become a better believer by loving my wife and watching her love me.

Love means learning to be broken. Kayla has needs, and I have needs too. I've learned that to love Kayla, I have to get in touch with my inner world. It's okay to not be okay. It's okay to cry. And in order to love Kayla well, I have to know how to reach out and get help when I am not okay—not just reaching out to Kayla, but also to others. I have mental health check-ins with a few other people I can be real with. We'll ask, "How are you? What's going on?" Just a quick text or phone call makes a big difference. To love, you must be in a renewed state of mind. Reach out and call someone when you're not doing well. Get help.

I've learned to see Kayla as God's daughter. How I treat my wife determines how God will treat me. Kayla is more than just my wife—she is my Queen, my business partner, my coach, and MOST of all, my best friend. If I am withholding love from her, or if I'm not being truthful, it hurts her. I see Kayla as the butterfly. She's smaller in stature. I feel like the buffalo pursuing this innocent, sweet, beautiful butterfly. A buffalo might look stronger, but they have restrictions too. Although a butterfly is small, it can go farther longer. Just so, Kayla has strengths I don't have. We can appreciate each other's strengths. In chess, a king can only move one square at a time, but a queen can move in whatever direction she wants, as far as she wants. That's true in life. Even though I might be a tough guy, I'm limited in other ways. Kayla has helped me to realize the importance of being honest about what's going on inside.

Love also calls for radical forgiveness. I had to forgive myself for all the ways I mistreated Kayla, and she had to forgive me too. Still today, other things come up where I have to forgive Kayla, other family members, or anybody else I may hold resentment toward. I strip down my pride and accept that because Christ has forgiven me, who am I to not forgive someone else?

Kayla's love has strengthened my faith. Watching her choose to love and forgive me when I didn't deserve it has shown me God's unconditional love and forgiveness for us. If my wife can still believe in me, even after all the grief I've put her through, then anything is possible. Even when I was unlovable and she couldn't see any desire in me to change, she still stayed committed. She left for a season, but she stayed loyal and allowed space for me to make changes. And then she took me back. She showed true faith that stood the test of time.

Like Kayla said, now we are eating the fruit

of what we planted. We planted brokenness, forgiveness, and faith. And we are harvesting love. Pastor Williams, who told us to respect each other, is now the godfather of our second child, Madison.

Whatever you're going through, know that on the other side of your breakdown is your breakthrough. Whether you're experiencing mental health issues, addictions, a divorce, a separation, or anything else, those struggles are not the end of your story. Focusing on the inner man will pay off. The best is yet to come.

Reflection Questions

1. Why is getting in touch with your inner self important for experiencing true love?
2. In your relationships, what do you want to harvest? What are you planting today that will produce the harvest you want?

AFTERWORD

A wise old prophet once said to me, the calling on your life as a king will not be centered on a certain amount of money, wealth, or fame. That will not keep you from going through the challenges you are meant to face to become who you are meant to be. Quit spending time in regret and spend more time taking calculated risks. You do not decide your future. You decide your habits. Your habits decide your future. Read that again. Now act accordingly. This year will be the year of miracles. NO MORE DELAYS and only uncommon favor! Your life is about to run over with unexplainable blessings!

NOTES

1. Morals

1. "How God Gets Our Attention" TEAM3 Ministries, Facebook, September 1, 2020, https://www.facebook.com/TEAM3ministries/posts/how-god-gets-our-attentionby-charles-stanleywhen-we-walk-in-the-spirit-alert-to-/762285874505049/.

ABOUT THE AUTHOR

Richard Yeargin is a highly sought-after transformational keynote speaker who uses his life experience and powerful storytelling to inspire his audience. Richard is no stranger to overcoming adversity as he had to overcome being a supreme athlete to enduring a critical car accident that had broken his neck and given him a concussion. This traumatic event temporarily stripped Richard of his mobility and changed the trajectory of his college football career, but he still found a way to push past the pain and surmount the rigors of obtaining his bachelor's degree. Shortly after, he secured his master's degree.

Richard used his adversity to propel him, affording him an opportunity to be awarded the Brian Piccolo award while continuing his football career. This accolade is awarded to an individual who exemplifies courage, loyalty, and a commitment to redefining leadership. Today, he is a thought leader in the sports industry and a well-respected professor on Clemson University's campus. Richard is also a career development coach, public speaker, corporate trainer, and life coach. Richard believes that regardless of the title, the mission is to change lives one encounter at a time.

If you are interested in a keynote based on *The Man Is Greater than the Brand*, please visit richardyeargin.com or email bookings@richardyeargin.com.